Lenin and the Russian Revolution

Steve Phillips

Series Editors
Martin Collier
Erica Lewis
Rosemary Rees

Heinemann

Heinemann Educational Publishers
Halley Court, Jordan Hill, Oxford, OX2 8EJ
Part of Harcourt Education

Heinemann is the registered trademark of
Harcourt Education Limited

First published 2000

ISBN 0 435 32719 4

02
10 9 8 7 6

Typeset by Wyvern 21 Ltd

Printed and bound in the UK by CPI Bath

Photographic acknowledgements
The authors and publisher would like to thank the following for permission to
reproduce photographs:

David King Collection: pp. 15, 19, 26, 29, 55, 69, 78, 93, 128, 148, 152; Hulton
Getty Picture Library: pp. 4, 9, 22, 157; Society for Co-operation in Russian and
Soviet Studies: pp. 44, 62, 67, 74, 88, 107, 112, 119.

Picture research by Elaine Willis

Author's acknowledgements
I would like to thank the following for their help, advice and support during the
writing of this book: Nicholas Wilmott, Christine Bragg, Ian Davies, Ged
Stephenson, Margaret Phillips and Brian Jones, with particular thanks to
Rosemary Rees and Nigel Kelly. I am grateful to Eleanor Cameron, Timothy
Mathews and Charles Chandler for allowing me to use samples of their work in
the assessment sections and for their comments on early drafts. I would also like
to thank the many students I have taught at Somerset College of Arts and
Technology, Worcester Technical College and Glan Afan Comprehensive School
who have given me so many ideas and such inspiration.

CONTENTS

HOW TO USE THIS BOOK

This book is divided into three distinct parts. 'Russia in Revolution, 1905–17' and 'The consolidation of Bolshevik Power: Russia, 1918–29' are designed to meet the requirements of AS Level History. Both parts give an analytical narrative of events to explain what happened during this important period of Russian history. There are summary questions at the end of each chapter to challenge students to use the information in order to develop their skills in analysis and explanation and to reinforce their understanding of the key issues. The first half of the book will also provide a solid foundation for students in preparation for the more analytical work expected at A2 Level.

The A2 part of the book is more analytical in style. It contains interpretations of the key issues of this period and examines aspects of historiography central to the study of History at this level. These sections should be read in conjunction with the relevant AS chapter. The interpretations will also enable AS students to extend their understanding of the subject matter.

At the end of both AS and A2 parts there are Assessment Sections which have been designed to provide guidance for students to meet the requirements of the new AS and A2 specifications when answering examination questions.

It is hoped, too, that the book will also be useful to the general reader who wishes to find their way around what is a sometimes complex but fascinating period of history.

AS SECTION: RUSSIA IN REVOLUTION, 1905–17

Context

> ### Key questions
> - Why was the Tsarist regime able to survive the Revolution of 1905?
> - Why did the Tsarist regime collapse in February 1917?
> - What problems did the Provisional Government face in 1917 and why was it unable to deal effectively with them?
> - Why were the Bolsheviks able to seize power in October 1917?

KEY POINT

The Russian Empire used the Julian Calendar, thirteen days behind the Gregorian Calendar used in western Europe, until 1918. Thus the February Revolution took place in March, using the Gregorian Calendar. All dates until February 1918 are given in the Julian Calendar, thereafter the Gregorian Calendar is used.

At the beginning of 1917 the Romanov dynasty, which had governed Russia for just over three hundred years, was in a perilous state. The Tsarist regime of Nicholas II was under severe pressure from many sides. Even before the outbreak of the First World War, the Tsar's government had found it difficult to cope with the strains caused by industrialisation and the increasing demands for political change. The Tsarist system of government was considered by many educated Russians to be outdated. The regime had survived an attempted revolution in 1905 but only by making concessions under severe duress.

When war broke out in 1914 the stresses and strains already present in Russia were greatly exacerbated by the sheer scale and duration of the First World War. By February 1917 government in Russia was in chaos and, under pressure from both opposition groups and his own supporters, Tsar Nicholas II abdicated. The country then fell into the hands of the Provisional Government.

From February until October 1917 the Provisional
Government struggled to control events in Russia. Its
power base was small and unstable and it was unable to
cope with the war against Germany and threats to its
existence by opposition from both Right and Left. By the
end of the summer of 1917 Lenin, the leader of a small
communist group known as the Bolsheviks, had become
convinced that the Provisional Government was finished.
In October, the Bolsheviks made their move and seized
power in Petrograd, the Russian capital.

The year 1917 was one of great excitement and disruption
in Russia, during which time the country had gone from
an autocratic system under the Tsar to a communist
seizure of power. It is not surprising that historians have
spent so much time trying to explain the momentous
events of this year.

1: Tsarist Russia, 1905–14: The death throes of an autocracy?

At the start of the twentieth century Russia was a country undergoing a period of considerable social and economic change. Industrialisation had started to take place and the resulting changes were to have an impact on Russia's political system. The Russian Empire was ruled by the **Tsar** and for nearly three hundred years the Tsars of Russia had been members of the Romanov family. Yet by the early twentieth century the pressures it faced, both inside and outside Russia, were to undermine the bases of its political system.

Although the fall of the Tsarist regime did not take place until February 1917, there were weaknesses in the system of government, exarcebated by the stresses and strains imposed upon it, which were evident even before the First World War began in 1914.

TSAR NICHOLAS II

The personality of Tsar **Nicholas II** was clearly a factor that contributed to the undermining of the Russian government and its effectiveness. Often described as charming but weak, Nicholas believed firmly in a system of **autocracy** – rule by one person, the Tsar. Indeed, Nicholas had stated at his coronation, 'I shall defend the principle of autocracy as unswervingly as my deceased father'. The Tsar, supported by the aristocracy, exercised his power through a bureaucracy, the army, the secret police and the Russian Orthodox Church, collectively referred to as the 'pillars of Tsarism'. By the early twentieth century this system had been shown to possess several problems. The aristocracy, who owned the vast majority of land in Russia, was very conservative and against any change which might pose a threat to their privileged position. The bureaucracy (government administrators) was inflexible and often obstructed reform and the army and secret police often caused

KEY TERM

Tsar The Emperor of Russia.

KEY TERM

Autocracy A system of government which involves rule by one person, e.g. the Tsar, who rules according to their own wishes.

KEY PEOPLE

Nicholas II (1868–1918)
Became Tsar of Russia in
1894 at the age of twenty-
nine. He was overshadowed
by his domineering father,
Alexander III, and this seems
to have made Nicholas a shy,
introverted man. He was
unprepared for ruling Russia
and tended to fall back onto
his conservative and
reactionary beliefs. He was
strongly against changing the
way the country was ruled.
He was a devoted family man
but a weak ruler, unable to
provide Russia with the
strong direction needed
during a period of important
change.

**The Tsar and Tsarina
with their haemophiliac
son Alexis carried by a
cossack.**

resentment by their harsh methods. The Church seemed
more interested in preserving its own position as a large
landowner than looking after the spiritual needs of the
people. However, the main weakness of autocracy was that
this system very much depended on the calibre of the
individual Tsar and Nicholas was not the best person for
the job.

Nicholas II became Tsar in 1894 on the sudden death of
his father Alexander III and as a result was poorly prepared
for the task of ruling. Alexander III had been a
domineering and determined man to whom Nicholas
provided a sharp contrast. Of those who influenced
Nicholas, one of the most important was his tutor
Pobedonostsev who later also served as his chief adviser.
Pobedonostsev was a **reactionary** who saw all reform as a
threat to autocracy and helped reinforce these ideas in

KEY TERM

Reactionary This term is
used to describe those who
dislike change and try to
resist it.

Nicholas. The other main influence on Nicholas was that of his wife Alexandra, a stronger character than her husband but just as politically inept. She was also a firm believer in autocracy. Thus there was little appetite for change at the centre of the regime. There was also little understanding of what was needed to be effective. The Tsar and his family had little comprehension of the world outside their palaces or of the needs of ordinary Russians. The reign of Nicholas got off to a rather inauspicious start, which provided pointers to Nicholas's style and its limitations. At the coronation ceremony a drunken and excited crowd stampeded on the arrival of Nicholas and Alexandra, killing over 1,300 people. Nicholas dismissed one policeman and then attended a lavish banquet in the evening. This was quickly seen, even by loyal subjects, as rather insensitive and uncaring.

Many other examples exist of Nicholas having a narrow focus on events. During the Russo-Japanese War of 1904–5, when much of the Russian fleet was destroyed, Nicholas's diary entry reads 'Had a nice picnic'. There also exists film footage from the Tsar's own cine-camera of the Royal Family having summer snowball fights with projectiles of cotton wool. All of this seemed to indicate a detachment from the real world of politics and the needs of the Russian economy and society.

The weaknesses of Nicholas as Tsar of Russia undoubtedly affected the effectiveness of a system which relied so heavily on one person, but character deficiencies need not have been fatal to the survival of the regime. What brought them into sharp focus were the changes and challenges occurring in Russia in the early twentieth century.

RUSSIAN SOCIETY AT THE START OF THE TWENTIETH CENTURY

The Russian Empire covered a vast area, one sixth of the world's earth surface, and had a population of over 160 million people. The bulk of this population, over 80 per cent, were peasants living in the countryside as labourers on the land. Most of this land was owned by the Russian aristocracy, wealthy landowners who made up 1 per cent of the population. There was an enormous gulf between the aristocracy and the peasants in terms of wealth. Until 1861 the peasants had been serfs, owned by the aristocracy as their personal property. Although they had been given their freedom in 1861, the peasants had to pay for it and for any land they received as a result. These **redemption payments** were to be a source of continued anger. Thus, the peasants remained impoverished, working plots of land that were too small to support a family. They continued to work as labourers for the aristocracy in order to make ends meet. Control over the peasantry was exercised through the 'mir' or village commune, an organisation of village elders that decided which crops should be grown and controlled movement from the village. Rural life had remained largely unchanged since the middle of the nineteenth century but its stability could easily be disrupted by harvest failures. Tension and peasant unrest were never far from the surface.

Industrialisation lagged behind that of the rest of Europe. **Count Sergei Witte**, the Tsar's Finance Minister between 1892 and 1903, had promoted industrialisation with some success. Even so, by 1905 it remained small-scale and limited to certain cities, such as St Petersburg and Moscow. Working conditions in industry were appalling even by the standards of the time and, with trade unions illegal, there were no organisations to push for improvements in the lot of the workers. Any organisations that were set up tended to be infiltrated by the secret police. Nonetheless, resentment amongst the industrial workers did lead to strikes in demand for better conditions. As in the countryside, the potential for unrest was ever present. The industrial workers, like the peasants, felt excluded from society. At the mercy of large landowners and employers, they had little influence over their own affairs.

Another section of the population that felt excluded from Russian society was the national minorities. Russians made up only 44 per cent of the Empire's population. The rest comprised a wide range of assorted national groups, which included Poles, Finns, Ukrainians, White Russians and the

KEY TERM

Redemption payments
Payment made by the peasants who had gained their freedom in 1861. As the peasants had been the personal property of the landowners they had to pay them compensation. The peasants were also required to pay for any land they had been given alongside their freedom. Redemption payments were to be paid over forty years but the high sums of money involved meant many peasants fell into arrears – a source of considerable resentment.

KEY PEOPLE

Count Sergei Witte (1849–1915) One of Nicholas II's most prominent ministers in the period before 1905, Witte served as Minister for Transport (1891–2) before becoming Minister of Finance in 1892. He promoted a policy of industrialisation and secured important foreign loans for investment in Russia. He advised Nicholas to give concessions during the Revolution of 1905, resulting in the October Manifesto. He was dismissed in 1906.

KEY CONCEPT

Groups opposed to the Tsar

Russian Social Democratic Labour Party A party which supported communist principles based on the ideas of Karl Marx. Although its leaders tended to be upper or middle class, the party aimed its ideas at the industrial workers in towns. The party split in 1903 into the radical Bolsheviks and more moderate Mensheviks.

Bolsheviks A small revolutionary group of communists, led by Lenin.

Mensheviks A communist group, more moderate than the Bolsheviks. In 1917 they were a larger group than the Bolsheviks, in terms of support.

Social Revolutionaries (SRs) A group committed to democratic socialism who believed in the right of groups to govern themselves, e.g. peasant organisations. They gained support from sections of the peasantry and often stirred up peasant discontent.

Liberals Those who wished to introduce democratic institutions, based on elections, to Russia. They gained support from the lower aristocracy, intellectuals and factory owners and traders.

Muslim populations of Central Asia. Some of these groups had a strong cultural heritage and were keen to promote their own national identity. Nationalism had the potential to break up the vast Russian Empire.

Other groups, which the Tsar might have relied upon for support, were also becoming disillusioned with the government. Some of the more liberal members of the aristocracy recognised the need to modernise the country in order to maintain Russia's position as a great power in world affairs. This was a view that caused tensions at court as many aristocrats saw change as a threat to their privileges. Students and intellectuals who had the opportunity to examine a range of political ideas were often deeply resentful of the Tsar's government. They criticised the lack of freedom and fact that political power was denied to all but the Tsar – there was no parliament in Tsarist Russia. At local level there were town and regional councils (*Zemstvos*) but they were run by the wealthiest groups in society in their own interests.

With the range of social and economic problems existing in Russia it is not surprising that there was a growth of organised opposition to the regime. To the **liberals** the creation of more democratic institutions, especially a national parliament, was seen as a key requirement. Other groups, such as the **Mensheviks** and **Bolsheviks**, both of which were Marxist groups, and the **SRs** (**Social Revolutionaries**) saw a more radical solution to the problem. To them the change would have to be more revolutionary. Support for these opposition groups was confined to a small, educated section of society but they represented the growth of tensions in society as a whole.

To maintain the stability of the regime, Nicholas II relied on the heavy-handed approach of the army and the secret police. Opportunities for peaceful change towards a more democratic system were limited by the stubborn, reactionary attitudes of Nicholas II, yet the pressures for change could not be contained indefinitely.

THE REVOLUTION OF 1905

The tensions that were present in Russian society were to come to a head in 1905 when a combination of factors resulted in a revolutionary situation.

The political temperature had been raised by a war against Japan in 1904. Plehve, the Tsar's Minister of the Interior, had recommended 'a small victorious war to stop the revolutionary tide' and encouraged Nicholas to expand the Empire in the Far East. This policy brought Russia up against the growing power of Japan and resulted in the Russo-Japanese War of 1904-5. It was an unnecessary war which ended in disaster for Russia. Japan seized Port Arthur and sank most of the Russian fleet. When a peace settlement was reached in 1905 the Russians were let off lightly but the defeat by Japan, a second-rate power, was a humiliation.

By 1905 there was considerable public anger over the war. The situation was made worse by an economic slump that resulted in food shortages in the cities. The industrial workers were badly affected and strikes and unrest developed.

The event that was to spark a full-scale revolution was to become known as 'Bloody Sunday'. On 9 January 1905, **Father Gapon** led a march of workers to the Winter Palace in St Petersburg to give the Tsar, the '**Little Father**' of the Russian people, a petition. Father Gapon, an Orthodox priest, was the leader of the Assembly of Russian Factory Workers, an organisation tolerated by the government because it had been infiltrated by the police. Father Gapon was, himself, a police informer. The march was attended by more than 150,000 people whose demands included higher wages, shorter working hours and free elections. Liberals joined the call for a constitution that would give political rights to the people and set up a parliament. The economic slump had resulted in a rise in unemployment at a time of food shortages and it was this combination that gave the march a high level of support in the city. When the marchers arrived at the gates of the Winter Palace the troops opened fire, killing over a hundred demonstrators.

Father Georgi Gapon A complex character: he was an Orthodox priest, a police informer and revolutionary leader. He led the Assembly of Russian Factory Workers and organised the march on the Winter Palace, St Petersburg, on 'Bloody Sunday'. Exposed as a police informer, he was hanged with a clothes line in 1906 by his former comrades.

KEY TERM

'**Little Father**' A traditional title used for the Tsar of Russia. The title implied that the Tsar had the duties of a father to look after the Russian people. The 'Bloody Sunday' incident of 1905 was to shatter this view.

Father Gapon leading demonstrators against troops on 'Bloody Sunday', 1905.

'Bloody Sunday' had two immediate effects. First, it was believed that the Tsar had given the order to open fire. This was untrue but the incident destroyed the idea of the Tsar as the 'Little Father' of the people and seriously weakened the loyalty of the common people. The second effect was to produce a wave of sympathy strikes and unrest grew. In St Petersburg and other cities workers' councils, known as **soviets**, were established to try to co-ordinate the unrest. All of the soviets were short-lived. The unrest was spontaneous and difficult for any group to control. The absence of many government troops, who were still in the Far East, encouraged some sections of the peasantry to protest against their own grievances. Fears of failing to meet redemption payments due to high taxes led to rioting and the seizure of property from the large estates.

Low morale and the painfully slow return of troops from the war with Japan resulted in some mutinies. Naval units, protesting over poor pay and the harshness of officers, mutinied at Kronstadt and Sebastopol. The most famous mutiny was that of the sailors on the battleship *Potemkin* in the Black Sea. The sailors killed their officers and bombarded the port of Odessa. In the general unrest, nationalist groups in the Ukraine, White Russia and Estonia started to demand concessions. Throughout the Empire the discontent was becoming serious.

Causes of the Revolution of 1905

Long-term:
- poor working conditions caused by industrialisation
- peasant discontent caused by poverty and redemption payments
- lack of political reforms
- repressive actions of the government

Short-term:
- economic slump leading to unemployment
- failure of the war against Japan
- food shortages caused by the war

Immediate:
- 'Bloody Sunday'

THE IMMEDIATE RESPONSE OF THE REGIME TO THE REVOLUTION OF 1905

In order to save the regime the Tsar was forced into making concessions. Witte advised Nicholas to grant a constitution and set up a parliament (Duma) and this was done under the **October Manifesto** of 1905. The manifesto agreed in principle to allow all classes to take part in elections. It also granted freedom of speech, freedom of religion and freedom from arbitrary arrest. The new constitution, with its limitations on autocracy, amounted to a revolution in Russian terms. Yet a limitation on these concessions was

October Manifesto A statement outlining a constitution that would set up an elected parliament and guarantee freedom of speech and religion. It was issued by Nicholas II under pressure during the unrest of 1905. The liberals saw it as a step towards democracy but the Tsar was to restrict its implementation. The **Fundamental Laws** of 1906 made clear the Tsar's determination to maintain autocracy.

also made clear when, in 1906, Nicholas issued the **Fundamental Laws**. These laws stated that the Tsar could suspend the Duma at any time, that only the Tsar could propose laws and had sole command of the armed forces. Trotsky was later to describe the Fundamental Laws as 'a whip wrapped in the parchment of a constitution'. The Tsar had granted the constitution and he could take it away: the autocracy was maintained.

The October Manifesto was a small and limited step towards a more democratic system but it was enough to reduce the unrest. The liberals were pleased with the concessions and saw them as a useful basis for further development. The cancellation of redemption payments helped dampen peasant discontent. An improvement in the economy helped take the sting out of the urban unrest and the return of loyal troops from the Far East enabled the government to restore order.

The revolution of 1905 is often referred to as the 'dress rehearsal' for the later successful revolution of 1917. This view can be misleading. The role of the revolutionary groups had little impact on the course of events in 1905, but for both the revolutionary groups and the regime there were important lessons to be learnt.

The Revolution of 1905 had been a shock to the regime but it had survived and had shown some resilience when faced with opposition. The armed forces had largely remained loyal and the secret police were effective in arresting revolutionary leaders. Government concessions had enabled the government to weaken the call for revolution. What also saved the regime were the weaknesses of the opposition. The unrest had been largely spontaneous and the revolutionary groups had been taken by surprise. There was no one group that had been able to co-ordinate the unrest and channel its different strands into one movement. Large sections of the peasantry, whilst discontent, remained passive and the peasant unrest was not as serious as it had been in 1902-3. The pressures on the government were limited by the short duration of the war against Japan. A longer war might have been fatal to the regime.

In order to ensure its long-term survival the government would need to bring about changes in policy to strengthen the regime. Repression would only work in the short-term. The underlying social, economic and political problems in Russia needed to be addressed.

THE TSARIST REGIME, 1906–14

After the shock of 1905 there were pressures from some ministers at court to make changes in order to guarantee the long-term survival of the regime. There was a choice between repression and reform. The most prominent minister in this period was **Pyotr Stolypin** who believed that some measures of reform and modernisation were necessary to strengthen the Tsarist regime. The Tsar and other ministers saw dangers in this approach and preferred to maintain the autocracy as it existed as the best guarantee of their power and privileges. Nonetheless, there were changes in policy during the period 1906 to 1914 in response to the Revolution of 1905. The implementation of these policies did, however, meet with mixed results. Russia was in a state of transition and this added to the stresses and strains already evident in Russian society.

The Dumas in practice

The call for a constitution with an elected parliament was one of the demands of the demonstrators during the Revolution of 1905. Any hopes that the constitution set up under the October Manifesto would be the first step towards **liberal democracy** were to be quickly disappointed. Witte, who had persuaded Nicholas to grant the constitution, was dismissed and when the Tsar opened the first **Duma** he announced his intention to maintain autocracy.

Elections for the first Duma, held in 1906, resulted in a parliament dominated by the Kadets, a group of liberals. The other main parties were the Octobrists, a conservative group that was willing to accept the October Manifesto, and the Trudoviki, a left-wing group with peasant support. There were also numerous representatives of the national minorities. Most revolutionary groups boycotted the elections. The Duma soon clashed with the government over the issue of land reform for the peasants and the rights of minority nationalities. Faced with this opposition Nicholas dissolved the Duma and called for new elections. A different system was used to elect members of the second Duma (1907) and this led to accusations of government 'rigging' of the results. Whether this was true or not, the result hardly pleased the Tsar as the second Duma contained more members from extreme political parties. This Duma lasted less than four months (February–June 1907) before Nicholas dissolved it.

In an attempt to produce a Duma more agreeable to the government, Stolypin decided to introduce a new Electoral Law in 1907. This law ensured that the landowners held 50 per cent of the votes and restricted those of the urban workers and peasants. The result of elections that followed was a third Duma dominated by the conservative Octobrists. Even this Duma was not prepared to blindly agree to the government's wishes and Stolypin often had to resort to using decrees in order to bypass them. Nonetheless, the third Duma lasted from 1907 until 1912.

Russia's experiment with a constitution had resulted in a bitter and frustrated parliament with little real power. The Tsar usually rejected any reform measures proposed by the Duma. Nicholas had therefore been one of the main obstacles preventing the Dumas developing into a parliament with any real power.

Industrialisation

Industrialisation, which had lagged behind that of the rest of Europe, had been promoted by two of the Tsar's most able politicians: Witte between 1892 and 1903 and, after 1905, by Stolypin. Industrialisation was seen as a way of modernising the Russian economy and, by generating wealth and making more use of Russia's resources, strengthening the Tsarist regime in the long term. There is no doubt that by its own standards the Tsarist regime achieved considerable success. The overall growth rate for industry between 1906 and 1913 was about 6 per cent per year with heavy industry growing particularly rapidly. Foreign trade also increased with both exports and imports doubling between 1900 and 1913. These figures show impressive growth, although from a small base. In the short term this programme of industrialisation produced problems of its own. It was only achieved by heavy taxation of the peasantry and it relied to a large extent on foreign investment. Although production of consumer goods rose, it lagged behind that of heavy industry. The rapid speed of industrialisation also produced tensions. Factory inspectors were few in number and this allowed employers to exploit their workers. Large industrial centres of over 2,000 workers, often working in appalling conditions reminiscent of early nineteenth-century Britain, provided a breeding ground for discontent.

Agricultural policy

In agriculture there was progress, with the land reforms put forward by Stolypin. **Peasants** were encouraged to leave the village commune and own their own land on consolidated farms. Two and a half million households took advantage of this. The aim of this reform was not only to improve agricultural efficiency but also to create a class of more prosperous peasants or **kulaks**, who would be more loyal to the Tsarist government. Agricultural production did rise from 45.9 million tonnes in 1906 to 61.7 million tonnes in 1913, although this was still inefficient when compared to the rest of Europe. In terms of creating a more loyal peasantry the results were mixed. Official statistics show a decline in peasant riots from 3,000 in 1905 to only 128 in 1913 but there is considerable evidence of increasing tension between the poorer peasants and the slightly more prosperous kulaks.

Developments in education

Improvements made in education could also be seen as an attempt by the government to reduce unrest and raise the conditions of the Russian people. The number of pupils in primary education doubled between 1904 and 1914, those in secondary education quadrupled and the number of students in higher education tripled in the same period. These figures indicate significant progress, but the reforms were criticised as being too little, too late. Education also made it easier to spread revolutionary ideas to an already discontented people.

KEY CONCEPT

The Russian peasantry A significant number of the Russian peasantry had been serfs (i.e. slaves, the property of rich landowners) until they were given their freedom in 1861. Most peasants remained dependent on rich landowners for agricultural work. They were controlled through the village commune or mir, an organisation made up of village elders. Living conditions were generally very primitive. Some peasants were able to own their own small farms and make a decent living. These slightly better off peasants were known as **kulaks**.

The growth of organised opposition after 1905

Given the subsequent events of the Bolshevik takeover, historians have focused a lot of attention on the role of revolutionary groups in the opposition to Tsarism but in the unrest of 1905, sparked off by the hardships of the war against Japan, the revolutionary groups were largely unorganised, small in number and divided amongst themselves. The period after 1905 saw a decline in both organised and spontaneous unrest as economic recovery took place. The **Okhrana** used ruthless tactics to deal with the revolutionaries. Stolypin set up field court martials, which resulted in the execution of 1,144 people in 1907. The hangman's noose was referred to as 'Stolypin's necktie'.

Although the industrial workers were more passive after 1905, it was clear that tension was not far below the surface. A strike in the Lena goldfields in 1912, when 270 strikers were killed by the army and a wave of sympathy strikes followed, showed how volatile the situation could be. Police and army action was often brutal, causing further resentment, which helped the revolutionary groups gain support. Nonetheless, it would be misleading to give the impression of a strong and well-organised labour movement. Trade unions had little influence outside St Petersburg and Moscow and in total only had a membership of about 31,000 out of an industrial

KEY TERM

Okhrana The Tsar's secret police. Their job was to get rid of opposition groups to the Tsar.

Peasants during the Tsarist period, 1900–14.

workforce of two and a half million. Strikes were common, with a rise from 2,400 in 1913 to 4,000 in the first seven months of 1914, but it should be remembered that most strikes were over working conditions rather than aiming to overthrow the government. The Tsar's secret police, the Okhrana, was successful in infiltrating a lot of these groups. Russia, on the eve of the First World War, was far from the brink of a workers' revolution: Lenin himself had stated: 'We will not see the Revolution in our lifetime'.

CONCLUSIONS

After 1905 the Tsar's government had introduced some reforms, for example in economic policy, which were aimed at strengthening the regime in the long-term. Yet these changes were to produce tensions of their own, as they were still heavily restricted by the confines of an autocratic system.

The tensions in Russia at the beginning of 1914, coupled with the weaknesses of Nicholas II, have led some historians to see the collapse of Tsarism as inevitable. Tsarism was perhaps an outmoded system given the modernisation of the economy and the social changes it was bringing about. But even weak autocratic governments can have a very long life. What was needed to bring the Tsarist system down was a catalyst and that was provided by the First World War.

SUMMARY QUESTIONS

1 Explain what is meant by 'autocracy'. Why might Tsar Nicholas II have been considered unsuitable for the role of autocrat?

2 What were the immediate causes of the 1905 Revolution?

3 What policy changes did Nicholas II and his government make between 1905 and 1914 in response to the 1905 Revolution?

2: What impact did the First World War and the collapse of Tsarism have on Russia?

The Tsarist regime was put under severe pressure by the challenges imposed by the First World War. The stresses and strains evident in Russia before 1914 were deepened by the enormous demands placed on the country by its involvement. The start of the war saw a rallying of support for the Tsar but as military defeats occurred and economic dislocation caused shortages in the cities, the survival of the regime was undermined. As disillusionment grew, even the Tsar's own supporters turned against him. By February 1917, faced with serious unrest across the Empire, the regime collapsed.

THE FIRST WORLD WAR

When Russia joined the First World War in 1914 there was, as in much of Europe, a wave of enthusiasm and patriotism which must have reassured the regime of its prospects of survival. When Austria-Hungary invaded Serbia, public opinion in Russia supported entry into the war as part of Russia's traditional role as protector of the Slavs. There was support for the war across the political parties, including the Kadets and Octobrists as well as from some socialists. The general acceptance of a ban on the sale of vodka showed just how willing people were to rally to the cause of 'Mother Russia'. There were high expectations of the armed forces as the Russian 'steamroller' moved into action. But this initial enthusiasm did not last long. Defeats at the hands of the Germans at Tannenberg in August and the Masurian Lakes in September 1914 quickly dampened the morale of many in the army. The war then brought many of the weaknesses of the regime into sharp focus.

Military mobilisation

At the start of the war the inadequacies of planning for military mobilisation were revealed. The armed forces soon suffered shortages. Rifles were in short supply and by 1915 the artillery was limited to two or three shells a day. Casualties mounted to nearly two million dead and over five million injured. One of the main causes of the shortages in military supplies was inefficient distribution rather than insufficient production and for this the government could be blamed.

By 1916 supplies to the army had been improved. The government recognised the importance of ensuring food supplies reached the army and good harvests helped in this respect. Unfortunately, food supplies to the cities were less secure.

The economy during the war

The mobilisation of the economy for war production was slow to take effect and the government had to rely on imports. Plans were implemented to gear industrial output to the needs of the war effort and substantial increases in production were achieved. Artillery production rose by 400 per cent in the first two years of the war. Yet as factories were converted to armaments production other goods became scarce. Fuel shortages also hit sectors of industry. The result was a rapid rise in prices. This inflation was accelerated by the government's policy of printing more money than its reserves could support. For those industries where production was high problems were caused by the inadequate transport system. Many areas of the country were still poorly served by roads and the railways were clogged by the movement of troops and their equipment.

One attempt to increase the production of goods involved the setting up of **War-Industry Committees**, made up of representatives of employers and workers. It was hoped that this would help identify problems in production and resolve them quickly.

To improve administration, the government set up **Zemgor**, an organisation to represent the town councils and regional zemstvos. The government gave it the task of

KEY TERMS

War-Industry Committees
Committees of representatives of both employers and workers to help sort out supply problems in the economy during the war.

Zemgor A body made up of representatives from town councils and the regional councils (zemstvos) to help co-ordinate tasks useful to the war effort.

A food queue in Russia in 1917.

co-ordinating additional medical supplies to be sent to the frontline and the organisation of refugees. The work of Zemgor was limited, however, by the tight restrictions imposed on it by the government. Even during the war the government was worried about giving away power.

The impact on society

The strains caused by mobilisation for the war were to have an impact on all social groups. The deficiencies in army organisation and supplies had a considerable impact on the peasantry who made up the bulk of rank and file soldiers. These peasants, suffering the hardships of the war, became much more radical and revolutionary groups began to find them susceptible to new political ideas.

For those peasants who stayed at home, conditions also became difficult. With young males conscripted into the army, farming was left in the hands of women and the elderly. The army seized horses for transporting military equipment, making agricultural work even harder. Much of the food produced was sent to the army by the government and the prices the peasants got for it were inadequate. Discontent mounted, fuelled by stories of terrible conditions at the frontline as soldiers sent news home.

The war also radicalised opinion in the towns and cities, where food shortages inevitably led to inflation, with the price of meat rising by 300 per cent and that of flour by 200 per cent. The shortage of food was not helped by the Russian 'scorched earth' policy whereby large areas of farmland were set alight to prevent food resources falling into the hands of the Germans. Wages for industrial workers had risen at the start of the war but they had failed to match the increase in prices. It was not long before strikes and protests occurred and, as with the peasantry, the industrial workers found themselves more in tune with the demands of the revolutionary groups. The War-Industry Committees had provided the workers with a useful platform for airing their grievances.

Even those groups who had supported the regime, and whose wealth might be expected to provide a cushion against the hardships of war, suffered. The landowners of large estates were hit by a collapse in the value of land and a severe shortage of farm labourers. Industrialists who failed to secure government orders for the production of war goods found the market for their products disappearing and many small businesses were forced into bankruptcy. Those companies that were given large government contracts during the war did well but they were seldom grateful to the Tsar. Many successful industrialists came to the conclusion that economic efficiency would be enhanced if the regulations associated with government intervention were removed.

As the war progressed there was growing resentment of the increased intervention of the government in daily life. The government found it particularly difficult to keep control over the remoter parts of the Empire and this provided an opportunity for the national minorities to assert some measure of independence. In Turkestan a major rebellion broke out in 1916 in response to the government's attempt to maximise conscription into the army. Thousands of lives were lost as the government struggled to reassert its control.

The impact on the government

The war not only revealed poor government planning but also the political ineptitude of the Tsar. The Duma was dissolved in 1915 and the Tsar made clear his view that he should have sole control over the conduct of the war. In September, Nicholas, under pressure from **Alexandra**, took over command of the armed forces and went to the front to direct the fighting. He was now in a position where he could be seen as responsible for military defeats and be the target of officers' criticisms of the war effort. He was also cut off from information about the situation in St Petersburg, now renamed Petrograd (St Petersburg was considered to sound too German).

With Nicholas away at the front, Alexandra was left in control of government in the capital. Already unpopular because of her German background, Alexandra further added to the demoralisation of the government by taking the advice of **Rasputin**, a holy man and confidant of the Tsarina. He was able to exert a strong influence over Alexandra because of his apparent ability to control the condition of Alexis, the only son and heir of Nicholas, who suffered from haemophilia. Rasputin used his influence to get both church and government positions for his friends and cronies and as a result upset many of the aristocrats at court who saw their own influence over the Tsar threatened. Ministers were regularly sacked. During the course of 1916 there was a succession of three Ministers of War, four Ministers of Agriculture and five Ministers of the Interior. The government was in chaos and the aristocracy, who made up most of its personnel, was beginning to lose faith in the regime as an instrument for preserving its power.

In 1916, Prince Yusupov, a member of the Imperial court who had become disgusted by Rasputin's actions, murdered him. Yet it would be wrong to see Rasputin as an important factor in the fall of the regime. His influence was limited and although it grew during the First World

KEY PEOPLE

Tsarina Alexandra (1872–1918) The wife of Tsar Nicholas II, Alexandra was more strong-willed than her husband and he became reliant on her advice. Unfortunately, Alexandra had a limited understanding of political issues and often acted on the advice of unsuitable people such as Rasputin. She was devoted to her children, especially her only son, Alexis, who suffered from haemophilia. Her unpopularity increased during the First World War when her German background allowed opponents to raise doubts about her loyalty to Russia.

Grigori Rasputin (1869–1916) A religious mystic who claimed he could cure Alexis, the young heir to the Russian throne. This enabled him to influence the Tsarina Alexandra. When Alexandra was put in charge of the government during the First World War he was able to exert an influence over political decisions. His influence, although short-lived, was highly detrimental to the government.

Grigori Rasputin.

War, he is probably best seen more as a symptom of decay rather than a cause.

Even after the death of Rasputin, the reputations of the Tsar and Tsarina continued to decline. Rumours that Alexandra was a German spy persisted and it was even suggested that the Tsar's failure to inflict military defeat on Germany was evidence of his own German sympathies. By 1916 the government, undermined by rumours and speculation, was in chaos and seemed paralysed by hesitancy and inaction.

The First World War had produced the hardships which fed discontent and revolution and seriously weakened the capacity of the regime to deal effectively with them. The radicalisation of the peasants, industrial workers and soldiers was to increase the potential for serious unrest. The war also alienated the regime from its own supporters. The aristocracy, who supplied most of the army officers, had suffered directly from the military failures whilst their landed estates rapidly declined in value. They were alienated further by the refusal of the Tsar to give them a meaningful role in the running of the country. Any reasons they had for standing by the regime were fading fast.

THE FEBRUARY REVOLUTION 1917

By the beginning of 1917 there were demonstrations in Petrograd over food shortages, which were increasingly aimed against the Tsar. The radicalisation of the industrial workers and peasants which had occurred during the war now became significant. Workers' councils or Soviets started to reform in the hope of taking advantage of the situation. The number of demonstrators rose to a high of nearly a quarter of a million in February when a strike at the Putilov works in Petrograd coincided with International Women's Day, bringing thousands of women onto the streets in protest at food shortages. In this situation the attitude of the army was crucial and key elements within it, including the Cossacks, refused to obey the orders of the Tsar and fire on demonstrators. The Tsar had lost the backing of his own supporters and under pressure from the army leaders, who were sick of the lack of progress in the war, Nicholas was persuaded to abdicate. The throne was offered to his brother who declined and the Romanov dynasty came to an end.

The end of the Tsarist regime had not been brought about by actions of revolutionary groups; it had collapsed rather than been overthrown. The long-term weaknesses evident in the regime had made it vulnerable to the additional strains imposed by the First World War. When, in February 1917, the regime was under severe pressure it found that its own supporters were no longer willing to save a government they had lost faith in.

SUMMARY QUESTIONS

1 How much support was there within Russia for the decision to join the First World War?

2 What measures did the Tsar's government take to gear the economy towards the demands of war between 1914 and 1917?

3 The photograph on page 19 presents an image of social conditions in Russia during the First World War. How useful is this source?

4 What were the consequences of Nicholas II's decision to leave Petrograd and direct the war effort on the Eastern Front?

5 Why was the Tsarist Regime so unpopular by early 1917?

3: What problems did the Provisional Government face?

After the February Revolution which saw the fall of the Tsar, a Provisional Government was set up. Formed from the Duma or representative assembly, which had existed under the Tsar, the new government was a weak and unstable grouping of politicians trying desperately to gain some control over events. Led initially by **Prince Lvov** and after July 1917 by Kerensky, the Provisional Government faced the same problems as the Tsar and was unable to offer any effective solutions. From the start it lacked both authority and support.

THE FIRST WORLD WAR

The war was the most pressing problem for the Provisional Government, who took the unpopular decision to continue the campaign against Germany, in the hope that they could turn the tide against the Germans and gain land. They also felt that by honouring the alliance with France and Britain Russia would get important financial support. **Kerensky** launched a major offensive against the Germans in June but the Russians made no headway and morale started to collapse. Desertions reached worrying levels with over two million soldiers returning home in 1917. This decision to continue the war severely weakened the capacity of the Provisional Government to consolidate its position and deal with the other problems it faced. It also showed just how out of touch the government was with the concerns of those suffering the hardships of war: rank and file soldiers, the industrial workers and the peasantry.

THE PETROGRAD SOVIET

What also weakened the government from the start was its lack of credibility and authority. It had not been elected and had no programme for government. The Petrograd Soviet had a better claim to legitimacy having been formed from representatives of the workers. It then expanded its base to include soldiers. The Soviet had considerable power, with its control over the postal service and railways in Petrograd, to the extent that it was difficult for the Provisional Government to do anything without its support. This point was illustrated by the Petrograd Soviet's Order No. 1, which urged the soldiers to only obey the orders of the Government if they did not contradict its own decrees. Kerensky failed to gain any real level of trust from the Soviet and had little choice but to tolerate it. This system of 'dual power' between the Government and the Petrograd Soviet added to the chaos of the situation but neither side was in a position to deal effectively with the other.

THE DECISION TO DELAY THE CONSTITUENT ASSEMBLY

One area where the Provisional Government could have gained support was through the calling of a **Constituent Assembly** or parliament to legitimise its powers and to introduce land reform, but Kerensky delayed the summoning of a Constituent Assembly. Although the rights of peasants to the great landed estates were recognised in principle, the Government was in no position to implement this. The grievances over land had long been a concern to peasants and many were unwilling to wait any longer. Many of those peasants who had deserted the army and returned home had done so in order to seize some land for themselves. The Government's failure to take a lead on reform lost it valuable support from the peasantry. Disorder spread to the countryside with many landowners finding themselves on the receiving end of the peasants' anger. The Government was clearly unable to control what was happening.

THE 'JULY DAYS'

For many industrial workers the months following the February Revolution were a time of great excitement and

Alexander Kerensky.

those based in Petrograd and Moscow were quickly becoming not only more radical but also more organised. This development posed a danger for the Provisional Government. Sailors at the naval base of Kronstadt organised their own armed demonstration under Bolshevik slogans such as 'All power to the Soviets' and marched into Petrograd in what became known as the 'July Days'. This posed a dilemma for the Bolsheviks. Middle-ranking Bolsheviks were happy to encourage the rising but the Bolshevik leadership hesitated and refused to endorse this attempt to overthrow the government. Lenin preferred to 'wait and see'. With support from the Mensheviks and Social Revolutionaries, the Provisional Government was able to crush the rising.

The importance of the 'July Days' was that it led, in the short term, to the discrediting of the Bolsheviks, who were blamed by many for the bloodshed. Kerensky also used this as an opportunity to attack Lenin personally by claiming he was a German spy working to undermine the Russian war effort. Bolshevik offices were closed, as was their newspaper *Pravda*. Leading Bolsheviks were forced into hiding; Kamenev and Trotsky were arrested. The role of the Bolsheviks in the 'July Days' has caused some debate amongst historians. The standard view of Soviet writers before the 1980s was that the Bolsheviks took little part in the events but some Western historians see Bolshevik reticence at being involved as demonstrating a lack of nerve in seeing through a serious attempt to seize power. For Lenin the time was not yet right for revolution. For the Provisional Government, the crushing of the rising gave them temporary relief from the threat of the Left though this was to be followed by a serious threat from the Right.

THE KORNILOV 'COUP'

The position of the Provisional Government was severely undermined by what became known as the **Kornilov *coup***. After the 'July Days' Kerensky made an attempt to assert control over events and appointed Kornilov as Commander in Chief to reassert discipline in the army. This measure was too reactionary for the Mensheviks and Social

Revolutionaries, who were now part of the Government, but Kornilov was hailed as a hero by the Right.

Even some of the Liberals now talked of the advantages of military rule. With continued strikes and unrest in Petrograd the Government edged towards the imposition of martial law. Kornilov moved to suppress unrest in Petrograd but at the last moment Kerensky ordered his arrest and had to call on the Soviet to help defend the city against what seemed like an attempted *coup* by Kornilov. The Soviet came to Kerensky's aid and Kornilov was arrested. What were the motives of Kornilov? Was this really an attempted *coup* or, as Kornilov claimed, was he merely following Kerensky's orders to bring troops to the capital to restore order? Kerensky's ambiguous role in this affair was to seriously damage his standing with both the Right and the Left. The army was left demoralised and confused with little sense of direction. On the Left, the affair led to an upsurge in support for the Bolsheviks, who had taken a lead in organising the workers against Kornilov, whilst support for the Mensheviks and Social Revolutionaries, both associated with the Government, declined. Kerensky and the Provisional Government were now dangerously isolated and drifting towards final collapse.

THE FAILURE OF THE PROVISIONAL GOVERNMENT

By October 1917 the Bolsheviks were in a position to succeed in seizing power from the Provisional Government, although by this time the Provisional Government wielded little power of its own.

It is difficult not to reach a verdict of failure on the Provisional Government; it had lasted little more than eight months. Yet it should be remembered that the country had undergone enormous political change in a very short time. From being a strict autocracy Russia had gained a liberal constitution which, in theory, many in the West admired due to its emphasis on complete political and religious freedom. It even banned capital punishment in the army. The policies of the Provisional Government had also included the release of all political prisoners.

General Lavr Kornilov (1870–1918) In the summer of 1917 Kornilov became a focus for right-wing forces opposed to the Provisional Government and its failure to deal effectively with social unrest. Kerensky appointed Kornilov Commander in Chief of the Russian army in order to restore law and order in Petrograd but when his troops marched into the city they were stopped and Kornilov was arrested. Kornilov's motives are still unclear. Did he wish to overthrow the Provisional Government and establish military rule or was he merely obeying what he thought were Kerensky's orders? Opposition to Kornilov was led by the Bolsheviks and the affair greatly restored their fortunes after the 'July Days'. Although Kornilov was arrested, he had highlighted Kerensky's failure to deal with social unrest and this weakened the standing of the Provisional Government.

General Kornilov (centre).

These were positive aims but, as best demonstrated by the failure to call the Constituent Assembly and deal with land reform, their implementation was poorly handled and often ineffective.

From the start, the Provisional Government had lacked both support and authority. Its attempts to pursue a moderate line were perhaps undermined by the lack of a substantial middle class in Russia, but it could have done more to gain support from the conservative elements or even from the moderate Left. Instead it tended to alienate both groups and as a result was left isolated. The decision to continue the war was perhaps a crucial factor, sapping the strength and diverting the energies of a government whose hold on power was tenuous in the first place.

SUMMARY QUESTIONS

1 Why did the Provisional Government decide to continue fighting in the First World War? What were the consequences of this decision?

2 What were the consequences for the Provisional Government of Kerensky's failure to call the Constituent Assembly?

3 How did (*a*) the 'July Days' and (*b*) the Kornilov *Coup* affect the position of the Bolsheviks?

4: How were the Bolsheviks able to seize power in October 1917?

It is, perhaps, tempting to see the Bolshevik Revolution as an inevitable conclusion to the chaos unleashed after the February Revolution. However, this view would give a very misleading impression of the situation in 1917. In February the Bolsheviks were just one of many socialist groups, with a membership of only about 20,000. Many of its leaders were in exile or under arrest and there were divisions in the party about the best way to proceed. Yet in October of the same year the Bolsheviks were able to successfully stage a *coup* and take power in the capital. The October Revolution was a direct contrast to that of February, which had been spontaneous and largely unorganised. The revolution of October was a well-organised and masterly executed *coup d'état* by a party which had skilfully aligned itself with the demands of the workers and peasants. It is clear that the Bolsheviks were able to put themselves in a highly advantageous position in a relatively short time.

The February Revolution caused fevered excitement amongst the workers, soldiers and peasants. The task the Bolsheviks successfully accomplished was to find the common ground between the demands of all these groups and articulate them in order to gain support. In doing so, the Bolsheviks gained support from a reasonably wide section of the working population and were able to organise this support in order to seize power. They were also helped by the general situation in Russia in early 1917.

WHAT FACTORS CONTRIBUTED TO SUPPORT FOR THE BOLSHEVIKS?

- It soon became clear that the Provisional Government was not in a position to deliver the sort of reforms that many **industrial workers** wanted and, as a result, direct action was seen as the only way forward. The demands of the industrial workforce arose from the hardships they

KEY PEOPLE

**Vladimir Ilich Lenin
(1870–1924)** Born Vladimir
Ilich Ulyanov in Simbirsk in
the Volga region of Russia to
a relatively privileged family.
His father was a school
inspector. Lenin's brother
Alexander was executed for
high treason in 1887 for
plotting the assassination of
Tsar Alexander III. Lenin
studied law at St Petersburg
and soon became influenced
by revolutionary politics. He
changed his name to Lenin
but after attracting the
attention of the secret police
he was arrested and sent into
exile in Siberia. He spent
many years abroad between
1900 and 1917 and wrote
extensively about the need for
a Socialist revolution. After
1903, Lenin led the
Bolsheviks when they split
from the Social Democratic
Labour Party. He was in
Switzerland when the
February Revolution took
place. He returned to St
Petersburg, arriving at the
Finland Station in April 1917
to a large and enthusiastic
crowd. Lenin became
convinced that the time was
ripe for launching a
revolution. After the October
Revolution, Lenin led the
Bolshevik government until
his death in 1924. He was
devoted to the revolutionary
cause and a master of political
strategy. Yet his obsession
with the Revolution also
made him ruthless in dealing
with enemies.

were enduring because of the war and the desire to gain
more control over the factories in order to improve their
conditions of work. The soviets, trade unions and
factory committees were the ideal vehicles for pushing
forward workers' demands.

- Yet the **limitations of workers' organisations** provided
an opportunity which the Bolsheviks could exploit. The
growth in support for the Petrograd Soviet made
decision-making chaotic and real power was transferred
to a smaller committee of elected officials, often
politicians rather than workers. This move was very
important in alienating the rank and file members of the
Soviet, who felt they were being ignored. This then
played directly into the hands of the Bolsheviks, whose
support in the Soviet was weak at the beginning of
1917, and provided an opportunity they were to make
good use of after July.
- **Trade unions and factory committees** also found it
difficult to deal with the rapid pace of events after
February. Nonetheless, these groups often formed their
own armed groups, known as 'Red Guards' which could
be of use in promoting revolutionary demands.
- The role of the **soldiers** was of key importance, especially
after the inclusion of their representatives in the soviets.
Although there is evidence that patriotism remained a
strong force amongst front-line troops, those stationed in
garrisons were particularly radical. It was to these groups
that the Bolsheviks targeted their propaganda, calling for
a separate peace with Germany to end the war.
- The **peasants**, who made up the bulk of the soldiers,
were also keen to see the end of the war but their main
priority was to return to the countryside and gain some
land of their own and with it more control over their
own lives. With the increase in desertions from the
army, as peasants returned to their villages to seize land
for themselves, this issue became urgent.
- The skill of the Bolsheviks was in gearing their ideas and
slogans towards these three groups – workers, soldiers
and peasants – and organising support to increase their
power. Support for the Bolsheviks was greatly increased
by their skilful use of propaganda. **Lenin's** arrival in
Petrograd in April provided a major boost for Bolshevik
morale. In his '**April Theses**' he described the

The Bolshevik Revolution, October 1917   31

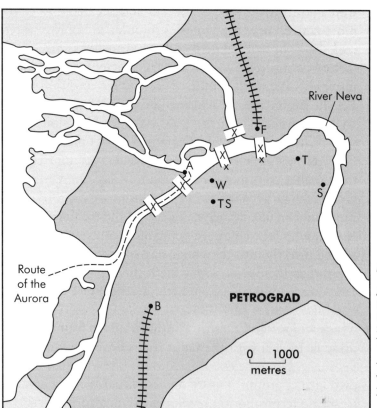

The Bolsheviks' key targets during the October Revolution, 1917.

River Neva

Route of the Aurora

PETROGRAD

0   1000
metres

Key:

A   Aurora Battleship
B   Warsaw station
F   Finland station
S   Smolny Institute, Lenin's HQ
T   Tauride Palace, HQ of the Duma
TS   Telegraph station
W   Winter Palace
X   Bridges seized by the Bolsheviks
▨   Built-up area of the city

Provisional Government as representing the bourgeois or middle-class stage of revolution which would move to a second stage of revolution where power would be transferred to the workers and peasants. He saw the Provisional Government as a spent force and advocated pushing for a workers' revolution. Lenin's promises to end the war, to give land 'to the people' and ensure adequate food supplies provided the useful rallying cry of '**peace, land and bread**'. This slogan also demonstrated the way in which the Bolsheviks were able to combine the demands of industrial workers, soldiers and peasants to maximise their appeal.

- Despite this growth in support there was the setback of the failure of the 'July Days', although this was temporary and in August the **Kornilov** *coup* revived Bolshevik fortunes, whilst at the same time undermining the position of the other socialist groups. The Bolsheviks' stand against Kornilov increased their support and gave them the renewed confidence of the workers. This quickly became evident in the September elections to the Petrograd Soviet. Trotsky became president of the Soviet and the Bolsheviks gained control. A majority was also gained in the Moscow Soviet. The Kornilov affair had also given the Bolsheviks a much stronger position in the Red Guards, now a force of 10,000.

THE SITUATION IN SEPTEMBER 1917

By September 1917 Lenin was convinced that the time was right to stage an armed attempt for power. Other Bolsheviks, including Kamenev and Zinoviev, were opposed to such an idea, arguing that a rising would leave the party in an isolated and uncertain position. But for Lenin the time was now right and any delay could lead to a downturn in their fortunes. It is here that the importance of Lenin is to be seen. He was able to persuade his party of the necessity for immediate revolution: a revolution which could be undertaken with the support of the Petrograd Soviet and the Red Guards.

What decided the timing of the revolution, however, was Kerensky's action. He decided to close down Bolshevik newspapers and arrest some leading Bolsheviks. Lenin and Trotsky then implemented the plans to seize power. Here the advantage of Lenin's insistence on a small elite organisation helped the Bolsheviks. Lenin's supporters were loyal and secrecy was maintained. The key positions in Petrograd were seized by Red Guards under the direction of a Military Revolutionary Committee (MRC) and co-ordinated by Trotsky. Power stations, police stations, bridges and the rail network in Petrograd were all in Bolshevik hands and with the help of a battleship pointing its guns at the Winter Palace, the Provisional Government surrendered what little power it had.

The chaotic situation under the Provisional Government created an enormous advantage for the Bolsheviks. Although the October Revolution was later presented by the Bolsheviks as an heroic struggle, including the storming of the Winter Palace, this was a gross exaggeration of the events of October 1917. The palace was not stormed, in fact the gates were open and very few casualties resulted. The Provisional Government held so

The role of Trotsky in the October Revolution

Trotsky was regarded with suspicion by some Bolsheviks because he had previously been a supporter of the Mensheviks. Nonetheless, his role in the October Revolution was of key importance.

- Trotsky supported Lenin's idea of seizing power through an armed uprising when other Bolshevik leaders were more cautious.
- He planned the details of the seizure of power in Petrograd. This was aimed at taking over key buildings in the city.
- He organised the Bolshevik Red Guard, taking responsibility for recruitment and discipline.
- He co-ordinated military operations through the Military Revolutionary Committee.
- He was a great speaker, able to motivate Bolshevik supporters to carry out their actions.
- He was an inspiration through his unflagging energy.

little power by this time that it was hardly worth overthrowing. Nonetheless, the Bolshevik seizure of power cannot just be put down to the weaknesses of the Provisional Government. Although small in number, the Bolsheviks showed themselves to be skilful at reading the situation and understanding what was required in order to gain support and seize control. They were thus able to seize the moment. Lenin and Trotsky had shown themselves to be masters of revolution but taking power was the easy part; holding on to it would be a much more difficult task.

SUMMARY QUESTIONS

1 Why were the Bolsheviks able to win support from (*a*) the peasants (*b*) the industrial workers and (*c*) soldiers during the summer of 1917?

2 What measures did Trotsky take to ensure that the October Revolution was successful?

AS SECTION: THE CONSOLIDATION OF BOLSHEVIK POWER: RUSSIA, 1918–29

Context

Key questions

- By what methods and with what success did Lenin consolidate Bolshevik rule between 1918 and 1924?
- To what extent were Lenin's economic policies driven by ideological considerations?
- What impact did the Bolshevik regime have on Soviet society and culture between 1918 and 1924?
- Why did Stalin emerge as leader of the Soviet Union between 1924 and 1929?
- What were the aims, methods and results of Soviet foreign policy between 1918 and 1929?

When the Bolsheviks seized power in October 1917 they took control of Petrograd; Moscow fell a few weeks later. Gaining control of the rest of the country was to prove a more difficult task. The Bolsheviks faced external and internal threats, both of which posed a serious danger to the very survival of the Revolution.

The external threat was that of Germany and her allies in the First World War. The Russian army was disintegrating and in no fit state to carry on fighting. Lenin decided that the war must be concluded quickly and this was achieved at a great cost by the Treaty of Brest-Litovsk. The internal threats to Bolshevik power resulted in a civil war between the Bolsheviks or 'Reds' and those who wished to remove the new regime, the 'Whites'. By 1921 this bitter civil war had been won by the Bolsheviks but consolidating all aspects of their rule was to be a slow process.

Much attention has been focused on the role of Lenin in consolidating the communist regime and bringing about change. When he died in 1924 Lenin's work was unfinished. Nonetheless, the Bolshevik regime had already made its mark not just on the political system in Russia but also on the economy and Russian society in general. Large parts of the old system had been removed but uncertainty about the future direction of the Revolution was increasing. Lenin had suffered a series of strokes since 1922 and while he was incapacitated his fellow Bolsheviks started to think about the future.

After the death of Lenin the Politburo was to provide a collective leadership but the period 1924 to 1929 was one of a struggle for power. By 1929, Trotsky, Stalin's main rival, and the leaders of both the Left and Right of the party had been defeated. As a result Stalin rose to become supreme leader of the Soviet Union.

5: How did the Bolsheviks consolidate their rule, 1918–24?

Seizing power in October 1917 had been relatively easy for the Bolsheviks; holding on to power was to prove much harder. After the October Revolution the Bolsheviks were merely in control of Petrograd. By November, fifteen main provincial cities, including Moscow, had fallen into Bolshevik hands. Other cities followed with a further twenty-eight under Bolshevik control by the end of January 1918. Yet it was not to be until 1921 that most of Russia was in the hands of the new regime.

The Bolsheviks had to deal with opposition so serious that it posed a threat to their very existence. The main dangers came from the external threat of Germany and Austria-Hungary and, within Russia, from opposition groups on the left and conservative elements on the right. Those groups within Russia who opposed the new regime were to rally together to form the 'Whites' and attack the Bolsheviks in what became a vicious civil war. By 1924 the Bolsheviks had dealt successfully with these threats and a measure of consolidation had occurred. This was a major achievement for what was a minority party. Yet the extensive use of terror and vast increase in party bureaucracy both pointed towards a regime which still felt itself to be threatened and insecure.

THE THREAT FROM THE LEFT

The October Revolution left the conservative forces in Russia in a state of shock. Kerensky tried to muster some forces to attack the Bolsheviks but failed. It was to take some time before the conservatives were in a position to make a fight of it, so initially the main danger to the Bolsheviks was the threat from the Left. Other socialist groups in Petrograd, such as the SRs and the Mensheviks,

KEY MARXIST TERMS

Proletariat The industrial workers.

Bourgeoisie The owners of factories, industries and shops, i.e. those who own the means of production.

Dictatorship of the Proletariat A government which rules on behalf of the proletariat. It would take over the reins of power and use it to smash the bourgeoisie and prevent counter-revolution.

demanded a say in the new government. They wanted what would have amounted to a coalition of left-wing groups. As far as Lenin and the other leading Bolsheviks were concerned there was to be no sharing of power. Relations with the other left-wing groups had not been good for some time. The SRs and Mensheviks had been strongly criticised by the Bolsheviks for joining the Provisional Government and the fact that the *coup* of October was a solely Bolshevik affair put the other groups at a disadvantage. As Trotsky had made clear to the SRs and Mensheviks: 'You have played out your role. Go where you belong: to the dustbin of history.'

Many of the other socialist groups thought that the Bolsheviks would not last long in power and refused to co-operate with them. This tended to play into the hands of the Bolsheviks as it left them with more control. The SRs and Mensheviks had misjudged the situation. Yet it was not just their tactics which worked against them. Divisions had also weakened the position of the Mensheviks and SRs. The Mensheviks were split into two factions; one led by Dan, the other by Martov. They did not reunite until May 1918. The SRs were also divided into a right wing and a left wing, the latter supporting co-operation with the Bolsheviks. One opportunity these groups did have to gain

---

Revolutionary groups and their attitudes to Bolshevik rule

The Mensheviks demanded a role in government, with the formation of a socialist coalition. When Lenin refused to form a coalition with other parties the Mensheviks decided not to co-operate with the Bolsheviks. Divisions between different factions weakened the Mensheviks.

SRs The *left wing* of the SRs supported co-operation with the Bolshevik government. The *right wing* were against working with the Bolsheviks, preferring to rely on their own support base. Unfortunately for the Bolsheviks, the right-wing SRs had more support.

influence over the government was with the calling of the Constituent Assembly.

THE CONSTITUENT ASSEMBLY

The Bolsheviks had criticised Kerensky for his failure to call the Constituent Assembly – now in power they were under a lot of pressure to keep their word. Lenin had a strong foreboding about this but felt it would be inconsistent not to let it meet. The elections were to prove Lenin's misgivings well judged. The results were not in the Bolsheviks' favour. They gained 175 seats in the Assembly with over 9 million votes but the SRs emerged as the largest single party with 410 seats and 21 million votes. To use the Assembly as a national parliament would clearly pose a threat to continued Bolshevik rule. To Lenin, the solution was to dissolve the Assembly and condemn it as an instrument of the bourgeoisie. In place of the Assembly, Lenin used the All-Russian Congress of Soviets as an instrument of popular support. It was, of course, a body in which the Bolsheviks had more influence. Not only had Lenin ignored the calls for a socialist coalition but he had also ensured that there was to be no real forum for opposition. This became more obvious when the other political parties were stripped of their rights and by 1923 they had all been disbanded.

THE TREATY OF BREST-LITOVSK (1918)

Lenin was quick to realise that Bolshevik consolidation would be extremely difficult to achieve while the war against Germany continued. He did not want the Bolsheviks to suffer the same fate as the Provisional Government and so needed to end Russian involvement in the First World War speedily. Peace was concluded through the Treaty of Brest-Litovsk (1918), which took Russia out of the war at a great cost. Russia lost control over the Baltic States of Lithuania, Estonia and Latvia, Finland, the Ukraine and parts of the Caucasus region (see map page 41). In all, this represented the loss of 32 per cent of Russia's agricultural land, 34 per cent of her population and 54 per cent of her industry. It was a harsh treaty. Why was Lenin prepared to accept this? It is true that some Bolshevik supporters were willing to fight on. The Petrograd workers were ready to defend the city against the Germans. The 'left Communists', who included Bukharin, promoted the idea of a guerrilla war of resistance. Other Bolsheviks, in the excitement of the period following their successful seizure of power, were ready to believe that the international proletarian revolution would spread to the rest of Europe and the forces of imperialism would be defeated. The lands lost under Brest-Litovsk could then be recovered. The Bolsheviks had promised to end the war before coming to power and to some in the party it would have been inconsistent if this promise had not been carried out. Yet, in the final analysis, it was probably the reality of the military and political situation which pushed Lenin into accepting the treaty. The Russian army was in no fit state to fight on. This fact was driven home by the German advance on Petrograd whilst the negotiations were taking place. Lenin was also aware that the Bolsheviks would face a civil war in the near future and resources would be needed for this. Nonetheless, Lenin had difficulty getting the Bolshevik Central Committee to accept the treaty and the decision was only carried by Lenin threatening to resign. This incident shows clearly the crucial role Lenin played in the shaping of events. The decision to accept the Treaty of Brest-Litovsk showed Lenin to be a realist rather

---

A summary of the terms of the Treaty of Brest-Litovsk, 1918

1 Russia would lose the following areas:
- The Ukraine
- Finland
- The Baltic provinces (Estonia, Latvia, Lithuania)
- parts of Poland
- Georgia
2 Russia had to pay Germany 3,000 million roubles in reparations to cover war damage.

Russia and the Treaty of Brest-Litovsk.

than driven only by ideological considerations. He was prepared to make compromises if it would ensure the survival of the revolution. The treaty also gave the Bolsheviks a better chance of winning the imminent civil war.

THE CIVIL WAR

Although initial opposition from the conservatives in Russia was limited, the Bolsheviks were attacked by the forces of General Krasnov at Pulkovo Heights near Petrograd immediately after the October Revolution. The **Reds** won this first encounter but it was merely the prelude to the Civil War. After the signing of the Treaty of Brest-Litovsk, opposition to the Bolsheviks mounted. This 'White' opposition consisted of a range of political groups. There were those who wished to see a return of the Tsar; liberals, including supporters of the Provisional Government; military leaders unhappy with Brest-Litovsk; national minorities seeking independence from Russia; and members of the Menshevik and SR parties who had been denied an involvement in the government. The **Whites** also received aid from the Allies in the First World War (Britain, France, the US and Japan). On the face of it, the opposition to the Bolsheviks seemed far-reaching but by 1921 the Bolsheviks had defeated the Whites and secured communist rule over the country.

Why did the Bolsheviks win the Civil War?

The Whites were an amalgam of different groups united only by their desire to get rid of the Bolsheviks. On what was to replace the communist regime they were deeply divided. Some wanted a return to the Tsarist regime; others a democratic republic. There was little in common between the Tsarist groups and socialist groups like the Mensheviks. The aims of the national minorities were more limited and often at odds with the White leaders. The slogan 'Russia One and Indivisible' did little to keep the minorities fighting for the Whites. These divisions were reflected in the military strategy of the Whites. Co-operation was limited, not helped by the long front on which the Whites fought (see map page 45). **Kolchak** established a government in Siberia but it had little contact with the forces under **Denikin** in the south. Thus the White armies fought largely independent of one another. Although the Whites were well supplied with old Tsarist officers they had problems recruiting conscripts. The peasants feared the loss of their newly gained land if the

(see map page 45)

KEY TERMS

The Reds The Bolshevik forces and their supporters.

The Whites Those opposed to the Bolsheviks during the Russian Civil War. The Whites were largely conservative groups within Russia who did not want the social order changed. Other groups, also opposed to the Bolsheviks, supported the Whites, including national minorities, liberals, and even some socialist groups. The aims of these groups varied and the Whites were to become very disunited.

KEY PEOPLE

Alexander Kolchak (1873–1920) A general who led White forces in Siberia during the Civil War. He set up a right wing government in the area he held. He launched a major offensive against the Bolsheviks in 1919 which failed and was captured by the Bolsheviks in 1920 and executed.

Anton Denikin (1872–1947) An ex-Tsarist officer who led the White armies in south-west Russia. He organised his forces with Cossack support and achieved some military success in 1919. By 1920 his forces were on the retreat and he resigned his command.

Allied intervention in the Civil War

Britain, the USA, France and Japan all sent help (soldiers, arms and money) to the Whites in the Civil War. Why?

- The Allies were annoyed by the Bolsheviks' decision to pull out of the First World War, as it allowed Germany to move the majority of her forces to the Western Front. The Allies thought that if the Whites defeated the Bolsheviks then Russia would rejoin the war against Germany.
- The Allies were capitalist countries whose governments saw the communist ideas of the Bolsheviks as a threat to their own way of life.

Allied support for the Whites declined after November 1918, when the First World War came to an end.

Whites won and saw the Reds as posing less of a threat to their position.

The Whites did receive help from Russia's former allies in the First World War but after the end of the war and the signing of the Versailles treaty in 1919 this assistance dried up. The Allied leaders may have had no taste for communism but neither did they desire to carry on fighting. The undemocratic nature of Kolchak's government also did nothing to inspire American help. At the end of 1918 there were only about 15,000 Allied troops in northern Russia. It is true that the Whites did receive money and military equipment from the Allies although not enough to have an impact on the course of the war. One impact Allied intervention did have was to make the Bolsheviks seem good Russian patriots against foreign interference.

In contrast to the Whites the Bolsheviks were able to organise themselves effectively for the war. Trotsky, who became Commissar for War in early 1918, turned the Red Army into an effective fighting machine. The army was

Leon Trotsky.

formed from the Red Guard units and pro-Bolshevik elements from the old Tsarist armed forces. Conscription was introduced to swell the number of soldiers to over 5 million by the end of the war. In order to get military expertise on its side the Bolsheviks conscripted over 50,000 officers from the Tsar's old army. To ensure loyalty they were paired with political commissars from the Bolshevik

---

The role of Trotsky in the Civil War

Trotsky was appointed Commissar for War in early 1919 and in this role he had an important influence on the Civil War.

- He organised the Red Army using 50,000 former Tsarist officers whose experience was called on to train the Red Army's raw recruits.

- He ensured strict discipline by use of the death penalty for deserters.

- His unflagging spirit helped morale at a time when other Bolshevik leaders were unconvinced that they would defeat the Whites.

- He directed the war on most of the major fronts, visiting troops and commanders to galvanise forces.

- He ensured that the Red Army was fed and armed.

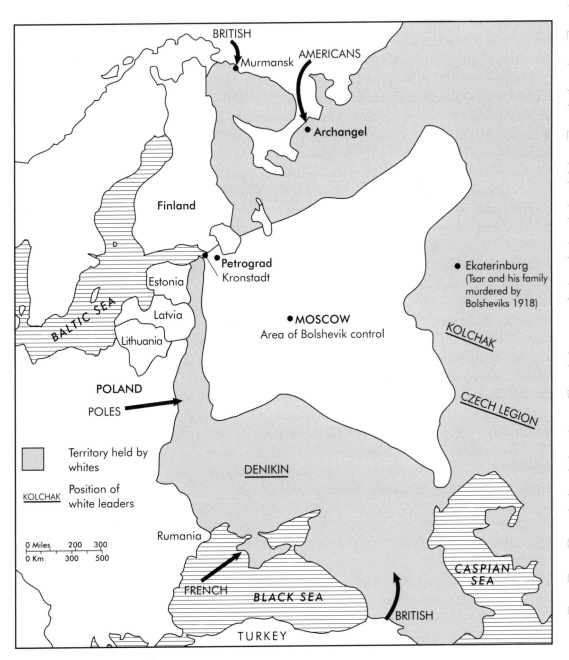

BRITISH

Murmansk

AMERICANS

● **Archangel**

Finland

● **Petrograd**
Kronstadt

● Ekaterinburg
(Tsar and his family
murdered by
Bolsheviks 1918)

Estonia

BALTIC SEA

Latvia

Lithuania

●MOSCOW
Area of Bolshevik control

KOLCHAK

POLAND

POLES

CZECH LEGION

Territory held by
whites

KOLCHAK Position of
white leaders

DENIKIN

0 Miles   200   300
0 Km   300   500

Rumania

CASPIAN
SEA

FRENCH   BLACK SEA

BRITISH

TURKEY

**Russia during the Civil
War.**

party. The Red Army became a disciplined, well-organised
and well-trained force.

At the start of the war the area controlled by the
Bolsheviks was small and being centred on Moscow and
Petrograd offered the advantage of ease of communication.
The rail network radiated from Moscow and this facilitated

the supplying of resources to troops at the frontline. The capital was moved from the more vulnerable Petrograd to Moscow where a large bureaucracy was developing in order to establish control over Bolshevik-held territory. The economy was geared to the war effort through the imposition of policies known as **War Communism**. Large-scale nationalisation of industry ensured adequate supplies for the Red Army (if not for civilians) and food supplies were requisitioned from the peasants. This latter policy was deeply unpopular with the peasants but it did provide enough food to keep the Red Army going.

By early 1921 all of the White strongholds had been defeated and Bolshevik rule had been extended across the country. Their military strategy had been more coherent than that of the Whites and their organisational skills were shown to be highly effective. A lot of the credit for this must go to the invaluable work of Trotsky. Yet it was not just better organisation that resulted in the Bolshevik victory. There was also a degree of active support for what the Bolsheviks stood for, especially from the workers who saw them as the best guarantors of their gains from the Revolution. The peasants did not like all aspects of Bolshevik rule but saw it as less of a threat to their newly acquired land than the Whites. Where support was not forthcoming force could always be used.

THE USE OF TERROR

The Civil War saw an expansion in the use of terror through the activities of the **Cheka**. Headed by **Dzerzhinsky**, this was a committee formed in December 1917 to deal with 'counter-revolution, sabotage and speculation'. The immediate problem it dealt with was looting but it extended its role to act as a secret police force and instrument of terror in order to help ensure the survival of the Revolution. The Cheka undertook mass arrests and executions, particularly in areas which had been held by the Whites. In 1919, over 8,000 people were shot. The most famous victims were Tsar Nicholas II and the rest of the imperial family at Ekaterinburg. Action was also taken against left-wing opponents such as the SRs and the

War Communism The name of a series of Bolshevik policies introduced during the Civil War in order to gear the economy to meeting the needs of the war effort. It involved large-scale government control over the economy with most industries nationalised (i.e., taken over by the government) and requisitioning of grain by force (i.e., taking grain from peasants to feed the towns and army).

KEY PEOPLE

Felix Dzerzhinsky (1877–1926) The head of the Cheka, the secret police of the Bolshevik regime. He was from a wealthy Polish background but used his powers as head of the Cheka to root out and destroy bourgeois enemies of the state. He was single-minded, dedicated and ruthless. Other Bolsheviks sometimes referred to him as the Shield of the Revolution. He died of a heart attack in 1926.

KEY TERMS

The Cheka The name of the secret police during the early period of Bolshevik rule. Replaced by the OGPU in 1922.

OGPU Replaced the Cheka in 1922. Dzerzhinsky, who had headed the Cheka, was appointed its leader to ensure continuity of function.

Mensheviks. When Lenin was shot in Moscow (August 1918) in an assassination attempt the use of terror was intensified. After the Civil War the Cheka was replaced by the **OGPU** and with this move came a change in emphasis. The use of terror became more bureaucratic and discreet; it also became more inward-looking. Attention was turned to groups within the party and large numbers were purged. Terror and force were also applied by the Red Army in the ruthless suppression of the Tambov peasant revolt and the Kronstadt mutiny of 1921. Estimates of the total number of people killed by Bolshevik terror vary but Robert Conquest puts the figure for the years 1917–23 at 200,000.

Many Bolsheviks were tough-minded about the use of terror tactics and felt they were easy to justify in the circumstances of civil war. The Bolsheviks were a minority group and, as such, terror was an essential mechanism for maintaining their hold on power. The state of war that they found themselves in seemed to call for forceful methods and although older Bolsheviks, often drawn from the intelligentsia, may have disliked using these methods, those new recruits who had joined the Red Army during the Civil War were less likely to lose sleep over this. The fact that the use of terror continued after the Civil War indicates a lack of confidence by Bolsheviks in their hold on power. The legacy of the Civil War was a long one. It had, in the words of R. Tucker, 'militarised the revolutionary political culture of the Bolshevik movement'. The use of terror became ingrained in the attitude of the party; a feature which Stalin was to make good use of later.

SOCIAL AND ECONOMIC POLICIES

During the Civil War the Bolsheviks did not have the time to set about persuading the people of the benefits of Bolshevik rule. Their policies were imposed on an already war-weary population. Nonetheless, it would be wrong to see terror and force as the only tactics used to consolidate the new regime. Social and economic policies were also used to strengthen the position of the government and to extend control over the population. They could also be a vehicle for compromises, which would at least ensure the passive acceptance, if not active support, of many Russians and thus help to secure the regime.

The unpopularity of War Communism was largely responsible for the Tambov and Kronstadt revolts, which shook the Bolshevik regime. These revolts were not begun by disgruntled aristocrats or Tsarist generals but by those who the Bolshevik government was supposed to be representing. Although the revolts were put down, Lenin came to the conclusion that concessions were necessary. War Communism was replaced by the **NEP** (New Economic Policy) which returned small-scale businesses to private hands and put an end to the requisitioning of grain which had been so hated by the peasantry. This marked a move away from communist ideology, with its emphasis on state ownership, and was heavily criticised by members of the party, but to Lenin it was seen as the only way of retaining a hold on power.

In social policy, attempts were made to reduce the power of the Church. Its role in shaping the attitudes of Russian people was clearly a threat to communism and the Bolsheviks were keen to remove what had been an integral part of the old regime. Despite wide-ranging restrictions on the Church and religious practice, the Bolsheviks found it difficult to completely eradicate religious worship, even if it was now confined largely to the home.

The Bolsheviks were quick to see opportunities for supplanting the existing mentality with that of a 'new soviet man'. Newspapers presented the Bolshevik line and the creative arts were used to praise the benefits of communism and the achievements of the new regime, although control over the arts was not rigidly enforced.

THE GROWTH OF PARTY BUREAUCRACY

By 1921 the Bolshevik party was much bigger than it had been in 1917. In the absence of virtually any other political force, many had joined the party to improve their career prospects in the new regime. Owing partly to the

NEP The New Economic Policy, introduced in 1921, allowed the return to private ownership of small-scale industries and put an end to the forced requisitioning of grain. It marked a move away from the unpopular policies of War Communism and was a response to the Kronstadt Mutiny and Tambov Rising.

Bureaucracy The civil
service (administrators) who
administer government
policies.

The Nationalities issue
The Russian Empire of the
Tsars had included many
different national groups who
had been incorporated, often
by force, into the Empire.
The chaos following the
Revolution had provided an
opportunity for these groups
to try to gain independence
from Russian domination.
National groups included the
Ukrainians, Poles, White
Russians, Jews and Tatars. In
the southern provinces of the
old Empire the issue of
nationality was also linked to
religious differences,
particularly in areas where the
population was Muslim.

circumstances of the Civil War, the party was rigidly
controlled and highly authoritarian. This authoritarianism
became institutionalised with the emergence of officials
whose job it was to exercise control. A **bureaucracy** was
inherited from the old regime and many who had served
the Tsar continued to work for the Bolsheviks. This, as
with the use of ex-Tsarist officers in the Red Army, did
worry some Bolsheviks although Lenin saw little choice in
the short term but to use such people with expertise and
specialised knowledge. In the meantime, lists were drawn
up of party employees suitable for certain jobs and
promotions were made by the party secretariat using these
lists. The party was beginning to form a class in itself
rather than being a vehicle for the industrial proletariat.
Lenin had realised the need for an administrative structure
if society was to be transformed and the party was best
placed to provide this. The soviets were assigned a
secondary role, emphasising the imposition of party
control over the proletariat. The party secretariat became
an instrument of centralisation, ensuring the country
followed orders from Moscow. The rising power of Stalin
as General Secretary was clear evidence of how successful
the party had been in centralising its authority.

THE NATIONAL MINORITIES

One particular problem faced by the Bolsheviks was that of
the national minorities, many of whom had offered
support to the Whites during the Civil War in an attempt
to secure some measure of self-government. Karl Marx had
underestimated the power of **nationalism**, seeing economic
divisions as more important. Lenin was to make the same
mistake. It soon became clear that some sort of
compromise was needed and this led to talk of the Soviet
Union as a federation of national republics. Despite this,
the influence of the Bolsheviks was weak in some of the
outlying areas of the old Russian Empire. The tactics used
by the party to gain control of these areas were to send in
Red Army forces whilst encouraging local Bolsheviks to
stage unrest. This policy was successfully applied against
Azerbaijan and Armenia in 1920 and, with rather more
difficulty, against Georgia in 1921. The Muslim areas to

the south of Russia posed more of a problem. The Bolsheviks were happy to encourage a separate Muslim communist party in these areas and guaranteed to uphold the customs of the Muslim community. Yet as the Bolsheviks became more secure in their position they watered down these promises and the Muslim areas were brought under direct Bolshevik control by a mixture of repression and compromise. The Soviet constitution of 1923 confirmed the power of the Communist Party in the state but did give some representation to communist members from each of the republics. The newly adopted name 'Union of Soviet Socialist Republics' (USSR) also emphasised the fact that this was formally a federal system. There was no mention of 'Russia' in the name of the new state. In the last resort, however, the Russians had the advantage of sheer numbers over the national minorities: Russia made up 90 per cent of the land-area and 72 per cent of the population of the new state. In addition, nearly three quarters of the members of the Communist Party were Russian.

By 1924 the Bolsheviks had been able to consolidate their position as the new government of Russia and extend their control over most of the old Tsarist Empire. This was no mean achievement for a minority group. But the nature of this consolidation had thrown up problems for the party, which were to have repercussions for the future course of the revolution. The use of terror and growth of an inflexible and authoritarian bureaucracy not only pointed to continuing Bolshevik insecurities but also laid the framework for future developments under Stalin. It is also pertinent to consider *what* had been consolidated. The proletariat had been severely weakened by the Civil War with the mass movement from the towns back to the countryside. The party which claimed to be representing this class was therefore in a precarious position. Had a 'Dictatorship of the Proletariat' been replaced by a dictatorship of the Bolshevik Party? Compromises, such as the NEP, were seen by some as sacrificing communist ideals. Was it the party which had been consolidated at the expense of communism?

SUMMARY QUESTIONS

1 Why did Lenin decide to sign the Treaty of Brest-Litovsk?

2 Who supported the Whites during the Civil War and why?

3 Why did the Bolsheviks win the Civil War?

4 How did the Bolsheviks justify their use of terror during the years 1917–24?

6: War Communism and the NEP: A retreat from an ideological economic policy?

As soon as the Bolsheviks seized power, economic measures were introduced which gave the peasants and industrial workers substantial control over their own affairs. These moves showed some commitment to creating the ideal world to which the Bolsheviks, through their **ideology**, aspired.

Bolshevik ideology was based on the writings of **Marx** and Lenin, who had adapted Marxist theory to the situation in Russia. Although the Bolsheviks had written at length about the evils of capitalism, their ideas on what to do when in power were rather vague. To Lenin the party must govern on behalf of 'the people', by which he usually meant the proletariat (industrial workers) but sometimes included the peasants. All land, factories and businesses (the 'means of production') should be seized by the state in the name of 'the people' so that wealth and goods could be redistributed according to need. Eventually social classes would disappear as greater equality was achieved. How and when this would occur was left unclear and this allowed a degree of flexibility when the Bolsheviks tried to justify their policies by reference to ideology.

INITIAL ECONOMIC POLICY IN 1917

Initially there were some radical moves to meet the demands of Bolshevik Party supporters and their ideology. The Land Decree of 1917 abolished all private ownership without compensation. Land was to be distributed to the peasants by land committees. This, in effect, merely legalised what, in many cases, had already taken place. The trickier issue of state ownership of land was played down at this stage.

KEY PEOPLE

Karl Marx Born in 1818 in the Rhineland of German-Jewish parents. He wrote *The Communist Manifesto* with Friedrich Engels, another socialist, in 1848. In 1849 he fled to London where he developed his ideas on class struggle and the economic laws of capitalism. He was writing at a time of great change due to the Industrial Revolution. His most important book was *Das Kapital*, which was first published in 1867. Although there were other socialist thinkers Marx was to have an enormous influence because he offered a clear programme of action. He believed that capitalism involved the exploitation of workers by factory owners and that this would not be tolerated indefinitely. Thus, according to Marx, capitalism would fall and be replaced first by socialism and finally by communism owing to the 'laws of History'. Marx died in exile in 1883 and is buried in Highgate Cemetery in London.

KEY TERM

Ideology A set of ideas which acts as the basis for an economic and political system.

In other areas workers' control was extended: in factories, the workers were to elect committees which would control industrial enterprises; in the armed forces all ranks were abolished and replaced by elected committees; and in the legal system 'people's courts' elected by the workers were set up.

On the surface, this appeared to offer greater freedom to the workers to control their own affairs, but at the same time government control was also being extended through the Supreme Council of the National Economy. It was unclear how compatible worker self-management was with government control and central planning. The role of the central government was to be greatly increased in the circumstances of civil war.

WAR COMMUNISM

The measures introduced to gear the economy for the war effort were known collectively as War Communism. All industries were nationalised and directed by the central government. Private trade was banned and food was requisitioned from the peasantry to feed the Red Army and ensure supplies for those in vital industries. These measures went along with the long-term aim of the Bolsheviks to abolish private enterprise and could be seen as the application of communist ideology, albeit rather earlier than the Bolsheviks had expected. To some Bolsheviks, the old world had been destroyed by the First World War and this provided an opportunity to build anew on Marxist lines. The collapse of the Russian currency and its replacement by **bartering** was seen by some Bolsheviks as a sign of the liberation from capitalism, when in fact it was caused by raging inflation. The result of this optimism was a radicalisation of policy pushing the Bolshevik leadership towards implementing large-scale nationalisation before it had originally intended to. There were also, of course, practical reasons for introducing War Communism. The Bolsheviks had inherited an economy which was in a state of near collapse and drastic measures were needed if they were to hope to fight and win the Civil War. State direction of the economy had been a feature of many

Bartering Paying for goods with other goods rather than money. This system of exchange is usually associated with undeveloped economies or where the system of currency has broken down. During War Communism in Russia it was seen by some as a sign of liberation from capitalism but was in fact a result of economic collapse.

European countries during the First World War and it had little to do with ideology. Some of the early ideas of the Bolsheviks for giving control to the workers proved to be idealistic and unworkable, especially during the emergency situation of the Civil War. The abolition of army ranks was reversed and factory managers had to be used to create some order in industry. Thus, there were several factors pushing the government into measures which extended state control.

Summary of War Communism

- Nationalisation (i.e. state ownership) of all industry, which would be controlled by the state through the Supreme Council of National Economy.
- The reintroduction of hierarchical structures in the army and industry. In factories the Workers' Councils were replaced by management in order to instil discipline into the workers.
- The forcible requisitioning of food from the peasants in order to feed the army and the towns.
- The introduction of rationing.

Tension between ideology and practical considerations was demonstrated by a range of issues. Government pressure to retain piecework rates in order to raise production for the war effort met with resistance from the workers, who viewed it as unfair. Rationing worked to the advantage of the Red Army and the party – a system that also led to some inequalities. The use of managers in factories (sometimes the former manager or even the owner was used) caused tension. The most unpopular aspects of War Communism were those which affected the peasants. They had little choice over the government's requisitioning of grain and Bolshevik plans to get rid of the **mir**, or village commune, were bitterly resented. The mir had been an instrument for exploiting the peasants but after the Revolution it became a genuine peasant organisation which most peasants wanted to retain. The Bolsheviks, with their long-term plans for state control over agricultural

KEY TERM

Mir An organisation made up of village elders which controlled the peasants and their agricultural work.

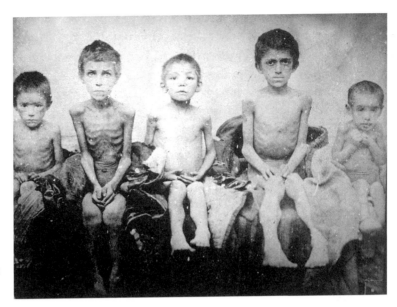

Victims of the famine of 1921.

production, represented a threat to the peasants. When the Civil War was over these tensions came to the surface and posed a serious problem for the government.

WHY DID THE BOLSHEVIKS CHANGE THEIR SOCIAL AND ECONOMIC POLICIES IN 1921?

The year 1921 saw a change in social and economic policies, which indicated a move away from the implementation of communist ideology, as the government struggled to find practical solutions to the grave situation they found themselves in at the end of the Civil War. Industry had ground to a virtual standstill. Production in heavy industry had fallen to 20 per cent of its 1913 level and in some sectors production had stopped altogether. Food production had also fallen, to two thirds of the 1913 figure, and the breakdown in the transport and distribution systems had resulted in widespread famine. Weakened by a lack of food many Russians succumbed to diseases such as typhus and smallpox. Over 20 million were to die from famine and disease. On top of this, army soldiers had to be resettled into civilian life. It was clear that War Communism was not delivering the goods, nor would it be able to cope with the situation post-Civil War.

The unpopularity of War Communism amongst the peasantry came to a head in a series of risings in 1920-1, putting pressure on the government to change its policy. There were risings in the important grain areas of the Volga basin, North Caucasus and Western Siberia. The latter involved over 60,000 people. The **Tambov Rising** in central Russia was a response of the peasantry to requisitioning teams arriving in the area to seize grain. The revolt was only put down after 50,000 Red Army troops were sent into the area.

Pressure on the government was increased in March 1921 when the **Kronstadt Mutiny** occurred. This revolt, by sailors at the naval base outside Petrograd, was alarming to the Bolsheviks because it was this group which had previously been a mainstay of the Revolution. They could not be easily dismissed as 'counter-revolutionaries', although they were labelled as 'White reactionaries' by Bolshevik propaganda. The mutiny was over the increase in power of the party and its officials at the expense of the workers. Its slogan was 'Soviets without Bolsheviks'. Sheila Fitzpatrick has described the mutiny as 'a symbolic parting of the ways between the working class and the Bolshevik Party'. The mutiny was suppressed by Red Army troops led by **Tukhachevsky** and under Trotsky's orders but the revolt was a shock to the Bolshevik leadership and was a key factor in Lenin's decision to change his economic policy. To Lenin, the Kronstadt revolt had 'lit up reality like a flash of lightning'. This pragmatic approach showed Lenin, once again, to be a realist willing to compromise ideology for the sake of ensuring the survival of the Revolution. As the political screw was turned tighter, concessions were made in economic policy with the introduction of the New Economic Policy.

THE NEW ECONOMIC POLICY (NEP)

The NEP was a series of measures which moved away from the tight state control of the economy introduced under War Communism. In agriculture there was to be an end to requisitioning, to be replaced by a system of taxation which allowed the peasants to sell any remaining food at

Tambov Rising (1920–1) A peasant uprising in the Tambov region of central Russia, which was sparked off by the arrival of Bolshevik units to requisition grain for use in the cities and the army. The uprising was largely spontaneous at first but the peasants were able to build on their strength by forming a Green Army and establishing control over a large area. It took over 50,000 Bolshevik troops to put down the revolt. This rising was the most serious of a series of revolts by the peasantry in 1920-1 against the policies of War Communism introduced by the Bolshevik government.

Kronstadt Mutiny (1921) The mutiny was by sailors stationed at the Kronstadt naval base against the imposition of orders from the Bolshevik government on the local soviet. The slogan of the mutineers was 'Soviets without Bolsheviks'. The mutiny was brutally crushed by the Red Army, but the affair was a severe shock to the regime because the sailors had previously been strong supporters of the Bolshevik Revolution.

Mikhail Tukhachevsky (1893–1937) A marshal of the Red Army and one of the key figures in its formation. Tukhachevsky was in charge of the troops that crushed the Kronstadt Mutiny.

Reasons for the NEP

- To increase food production by giving the peasants an incentive to grow more.
- To get the economy going again after the chaos of the Civil War. An element of private ownership would provide an incentive for small businesses and help increase industrial production and trade.
- To reduce opposition to the Bolsheviks and quell unrest, such as the Tambov Rising and Kronstadt Mutiny.
- To relax economic policies, especially the unpopular measures associated with War Communism.

market for a profit. The Bolsheviks also announced that there would be no forced programme of collectivisation. These measures were clearly a compromise with the peasantry but the Bolsheviks knew that without increased food production the economy would never be able to revive.

In industry the NEP returned small-scale industry to private hands although the state kept control of heavy industry, transport and the banks. This allowed Lenin to claim that the party still held 'the commanding heights of the economy'. In state-owned factories piecework and bonuses were used to try to raise production. To some Bolsheviks these were the techniques of the capitalist. The reintroduction of money was also seen as the re-emergence of capitalism. Yet the legalisation of private trading seemed the logical way of stopping a growing black market, a factor which had already led to some local authorities allowing private trade.

Results

From a communist standpoint, the NEP, with its acceptance of private industry and private trade, represented a retreat back to capitalism. The left-wing Bolsheviks were particularly hostile to this watering down of policy but, to Lenin, the Bolsheviks were in desperate economic circumstances and needed to make compromises to secure the Revolution. The NEP was seen as a short-term remedy. The economy would have to be restored before moving to socialism, as Lenin stated 'One step backwards, two steps forward'.

The fears of the Left were soon realised with the development of groups who gained under the NEP – private trade and small businesses led to the growth of the so-called **Nepmen**, those who used the concessions of the NEP to make money. The concessions with the peasantry were seen to encourage the kulaks to make profits from selling surplus grain. These groups were to become detested by the Left as capitalists holding back the development of socialism.

KEY TERM

Nepmen A term of abuse used by Bolsheviks to describe those private business people and traders who profited from the NEP.

The introduction of the NEP also coincided with the arrest of many Mensheviks and all political parties other than the Bolsheviks were outlawed. Economic compromise clearly did not extend to political relaxation, a factor which persuaded many left-wing Bolsheviks that the NEP could be tolerated in the short term. Bukharin, a left-wing Bolshevik, was to become one of the NEP's strongest supporters.

Although the NEP was criticised by groups within the Bolshevik Party, it was a policy which enabled the Russian

Views of the NEP

The Left Wing of the Bolshevik Party saw the NEP as a betrayal of the communist ideals of the Revolution. They disliked the reintroduction of capitalist elements such as private ownership and private trade and the failure of the government to collectivise agriculture. The NEP could only be tolerated as a short-term measure.

The Right Wing of the Bolshevik Party saw the NEP as a necessary step to ensure that the economy recovered and the Bolshevik Party remained in power. This would have to occur before moving towards a more socialist system. Thus, the Right also saw the NEP as a short-term measure.

Russian production figures, 1913–24. (Taken from A. Nove, 'An Economic History of the USSR'.)

	1913	1921	1922	1923	1924
Grain (million tons)	81.6	37.6	50.3	56.6	51.4
Pig iron (million tons)	4.2	0.1	0.2	0.3	0.75
Electricity (million Kwh)	1.9	0.5	0.8	1.1	1.5
Steel (million tons)	4.2	0.2	0.4	0.7	1.1
Cotton (million metres)	2582	105	349	691	963

economy to recover gradually (see the table). Under the NEP the peasants were more inclined to grow the much-needed food surpluses and, in industry, incentives encouraged the workforce to increase productivity. The NEP also took away some of the main causes of discontent with the Bolshevik government's policies. As the NEP produced a stabilised economy which started to grind back into action, Lenin was able to deal more effectively with any criticisms from within his own party.

SUMMARY QUESTIONS

1 What economic measures did the Bolsheviks introduce under War Communism?

2 Why was the NEP introduced in 1921?

3 Why did some Bolsheviks oppose the NEP?

4 How successful was the NEP by 1924?

7: Soviet society and culture under Lenin: Control or tradition?

The Bolshevik government used its position of power to attempt to change society, and so mould attitudes amongst the population and consolidate the Revolution. Russian society in 1917 was already in a state of flux owing to the impact of the First World War but traditional values stemming from Tsarist times were nevertheless deeply embedded.

THE POSITION OF WOMEN AND THE FAMILY

The **emancipation** of women had been a goal of most Russian radicals since the middle of the nineteenth century and the position of women was one area where the Bolsheviks made significant progress on coming to power. To more radical Bolsheviks the family was an outdated institution which deserved to be swept away. In reality, however, the complete destruction of the traditional family was never a serious policy. This is not to say there were no attacks on the traditional idea of the family. Youth groups were encouraged to attack the 'capitalist tyranny of parents' and party sections were set up to educate women members to become more assertive and independent. Wives were encouraged to refuse obedience to their husbands. Led by the Bolshevik **Alexandra Kollontai**, there were calls for greater sexual freedom for women. To young, radical Bolsheviks 'free love' was taken to mean casual sex and many considered it to be a right they were entitled to. These attitudes were shocking to older, more traditional Bolsheviks, including Lenin, and attempts were made to impose a more restrained attitude. Other attempts to remould the family consisted of an encouragement for communal spaces in housing blocks. Communal living by several families would break down the traditional family unit.

Emancipation The process of setting free groups or individuals. In respect to the role of women, Russian laws had given women a position which was subordinate to men. Russian radicals wished to change this by giving women greater rights and equality under the law.

Alexandra Kollontai (1872–1952) A leading Bolshevik figure in the early years of the regime, she was the first woman to be a member of a government in Europe. Kollontai was a feminist and believer in free love, a view which upset some more conservative Bolsheviks. As a member of the Central Committee she was able to exercise an influence on policies towards women, the family and health. Her influence waned after 1921 and some of her measures were reversed.

HEINEMANN ADVANCED HISTORY

Measures specifically targeted at women were also to have an impact on the family. Women were given a range of new rights and freedoms including rights within marriage. The Bolsheviks' Family Code of 1918 made divorce easier. A marriage could be dissolved at the request of either the husband or the wife without the need to give grounds, such as adultery or cruelty. Abortion was made legal and crèches were encouraged. Although these reforms were driven partly by a need to get more women into work during the Civil War, they were also an attack on the traditional oppression and maltreatment of women.

These measures had some success. The urban population made use of the opportunities to divorce and have abortions. By the mid-1920s Russia's divorce rate was the highest in Europe and abortion became commonplace in the cities. Yet these attempts to change the role of the family and the position of women also gave rise to some worrying features. The rise in the divorce rate did little to help women support children: few received financial support from the father of their child. The laws giving women equal rights in employment and equal pay were slow to have an impact.

It was impossible to change traditional attitudes to the family and the role of women overnight. Particularly resistant to change were the Muslim areas of Central Asia, where the **polygamous**, male-dominated family was well entrenched. Despite these limitations the Revolution did bring about greater acceptance of equality and Alexandra Kollontai was able to promote ideas such as the sexual needs of women, views which were very liberal for the time.

Measures aimed at improving the position of women were driven partly by ideological considerations – communist ideas of equality between the sexes. But there was also the more practical need to get women into work during the Civil War. The importance of practical needs over ideology is shown by the reversal of many reforms after the Civil War was over. Attitudes became more conventional, with abortion criticised and restricted by law. In politics women

Polygamy The custom of men having more than one wife. This custom was a central part of Muslim culture in the Central Asian areas of Russia.

A propoganda poster for the role of women in Bolshevik Russia.

represented a small percentage of the party's elite although it was an improvement on the pre-revolutionary situation.

RELIGION AND THE POSITION OF THE CHURCH

This was one aspect of social policy where radical change *was* brought about. To the Bolsheviks the Church provided an alternative ideology to that of Marxism. The **Russian Church** had also been an instrument of social control by the old regime; the Tsar had been head of the Orthodox Church. The Russian Orthodox Church had been the church of the vast majority of the population and was an important element in national identity. It was, therefore, a large task the Bolsheviks set themselves when

KEY CONCEPT

The Russian Church The Russian Orthodox Church had been closely connected to the Tsarist regime. The Tsar had been the head of the Church and used it to serve the purposes of the state. Appointments were subject to the approval of the Tsar and ensured that it would support the government and its policies. The religious hierarchy was headed by the **Patriarch**. The hold of the Church over the rural population was an important instrument in social control. As an organisation the Church owned a considerable amount of land and therefore tended to have the same interests as the landed classes. It was, therefore, both Tsarist and deeply conservative in its attitudes.

they aimed to destroy the Church and religion in general. There was to be no 'opium of the masses' other than communism.

A series of measures was introduced to severely limit the power and influence of religion. In 1918, the Decree on Freedom of Conscience separated the Orthodox Church from the state and the Church lost its privileged status. It was deprived of its land without compensation, its publications outlawed and all religious education outside the home was banned. A large number of churches were destroyed or converted to other purposes. The government closed all monasteries and by the end of 1918 the **Patriarch**, Tikhon, was under house arrest. During the famine of the Civil War attacks on the Church increased and valuable objects were seized to help pay for food supplies.

These policies were to severely restrict the Orthodox Church but failed to stamp out its influence completely. Surveys of the peasantry in the mid-1920s revealed that 55 per cent were still active Christians. Some of the attacks launched by the Bolsheviks met with resistance and demonstrated the continuing support for the Church. When the Civil War was over the Bolsheviks adopted softer methods for reducing Church influence. The focus was on propaganda which ridiculed religion for being little more than a collection of superstitions. The Bolshevik-sponsored League of the Militant Godless was active in spreading misinformation.

Despite the harsh vocal attacks on all forms of religion, in practice at local level there was often a more lenient approach. In Smolensk the local party branch decided that belief in God was not incompatible with party membership. The Bolsheviks were also wary of direct attacks against Islam and Muslim traditions were left in peace. The Bolsheviks seemed to lack confidence in their ability to take on the powerful religious traditions of Central Asia. Thus, despite the anti-religious climate under the Bolshevik regime, religious worship continued albeit on a much smaller scale. More importantly, the influence of the Orthodox Church as an organisation had been broken.

POPULAR CULTURE AND THE ARTS

The Bolshevik Revolution was to have an enormous impact on all sectors of life, bringing about important changes to the institutions and traditions which had existed under the Tsarist regime. Russia had a long and distinguished cultural tradition before 1917 although the role of **'high' culture** in society was limited to a small section of the educated elite. The Bolsheviks, whilst not seeing culture as a priority in 1917, did have some ideas on how it could be used for political advantage but their impact was mixed. The Revolution had produced a range of pressures, from radical experimentation with new ideas to more conservative tastes, which were often pushing in different directions. By 1924, **popular culture** and the arts were in a state of flux.

The last years of Tsarist Russia

The Bolsheviks inherited a cultural scene that was already in a state of flux. The last years of the Tsarist regime had produced great artists, such as the composer Stravinsky, the dancers Nijinsky and Anna Pavlova and the theatre director Stanislavsky. (Stanislavsky will be familiar to students of Drama for his development of Method Acting, where the whole body is used to develop characterisation.)

Modernism was having an increasing influence before 1917, especially in art. With its greater use of abstract symbolism, Modernism was challenging the more dominant approach of realistic representation. Linked to movements in the West, there was a greater desire to experiment with the limits of art and literature but even so these developments were only to have an impact on a small, elite audience. They had little effect on the mass reading public, now growing at a considerable rate owing to trends in primary education and the growth of newspapers. Many new writers were viewed as self-indulgent and out of touch with the needs of the population.

Nonetheless, there was enough talent and creativity to pose both an opportunity and a threat to the new regime. Despite some censorship, a degree of freedom of expression had allowed artists to use their craft as a vehicle for

KEY CONCEPTS

'High' culture This term is used to refer to those art forms, such as ballet, opera and fine art, which are geared towards a restricted and exclusive audience. The Bolsheviks disliked 'high' culture, seeing it as 'bourgeois' art.

Popular culture Refers to those art forms which are geared towards the general population and a mass audience. Popular fiction, the radio and cinema are usually placed in this category, which is sometimes referred to as 'low' culture.

Modernism A movement in the arts which made use of abstract symbolism rather than realistic representation.

criticising the Tsarist system and its values. It was this freedom of expression which was to become a worry to the new Bolshevik government, anxious as it was to hold on to power in the face of criticism.

Bolshevik attitudes towards the arts and popular culture

In 1917 the Bolshevik Party was divided over the importance and direction of cultural policy. Two views were prominent:

1 According to Lenin, culture was vital but subordinate to class conflict and the retention of power. Lenin's cultural tastes were conservative with a liking for classical Russian culture. He saw a desire for the party to keep high calibre writers and artists on side as much as possible. One important development Lenin implemented early after the seizure of power was to create a Commissariat of Enlightenment, a ministry of culture, to support and encourage artists. This was a development welcomed by artists as it replaced the traditional system of patronage that had centred on the Tsar. After the restrictions and censorship of the old regime many artists were encouraged by Bolshevik policies, especially as Lenin seemed prepared to accommodate those artists who were not communists but who were sympathetic to the ideals of the Revolution and who found plenty of material for their work in the events of the period. These artists were labelled by Trotsky as 'Fellow Travellers'.

2 The second view of the role of culture in the Revolution was that of Alexander Bogdanov, the Bolshevik intellectual, who argued that the state needed to use new technology to create its own 'Proletarian Culture'. Bogdanov believed a new group of proletarian artists should be assembled, for whom art was to serve a social and political purpose. This group became known as the **Constructivists**, aiming to create a new socialist culture. Workers and peasants were encouraged to produce their own culture, from writing their own stories to putting on theatre productions. This was a direct challenge to 'high culture' and it became popular for a time but by the early 1920s the government was concerned at the variety of

KEY TERMS

'Fellow Travellers' A term applied to those artists who, whilst not being communists, were sympathetic to the ideas of communism.

Constructivists Those who wished to create a new proletarian culture based on the worker and industrial technology.

viewpoints expressed through this culture 'from below' and started to impose restrictions on it.

The impact of the Bolshevik Revolution on popular culture and the arts

- In art many of the traditional assumptions were challenged. This was as much a result of the First World War sweeping away the old order as it was of the new government. The influence of Modernism was coupled with that of **Futurism** as artists attempted to convey visions of a new futuristic world. In poster art the Bolshevik regime was to acquire the services of one of the greatest writers, **V. Mayakovsky**, who set to work producing slogans and posters for the government. His work may have been propaganda but it was genuinely innovative. In painting and sculpture K. Malevich and V. Kandinsky represent examples of Fellow Travellers who produced a large output of experimental work in the early 1920s. Constructivists such as **Vladimir Tatlin** produced art which focused on machines of the future and ordinary objects which represented the nobility of labour (see Tatlin's Tower on page 67). This was an attempt to raise the status of workers and peasants as part of socialist values. It is not surprising that in a country where literacy rates were low the Bolsheviks put so much stress on visual arts.
- Given the economic difficulties of the First World War and the Civil War there were not the resources to build. This slowed down progress in architecture but plans showed a vision of the future which was both imaginative and diverse. Garden cities and high-rise apartments were among the projects designed in the early 1920s. The emphasis was, as in much of the art, on a functional world of the future: art should be useful to society.
- In literature the best work was produced by Fellow Travellers such as the novelist **M. Sholokhov** (*And Quiet Flows the Don*, an epic set during the Civil War), the poet **Anna Akhmatova** and satirist E. Zamyatin, whose *We* (1920) envisaged a regimented society where people were identified only by numbers. Literature could be

Tatlin's Tower to the Third International.

used to criticise the government as well as support it. In popular fiction the influence of Futurists was shown by an emphasis on science fiction.

- The theatre was largely behind the revolutionary aims of the Bolsheviks and rallied to the cause. V. Meyerhold produced the pageant *Mystery Bouffe* (1918) which showed the workers defeating their exploiters. The anniversary of the Revolution in 1920 was celebrated by a re-enactment of the storming of the Winter Palace using over 8,000 people. Parades through Red Square in Moscow were to be organised on a scale that made them examples of street theatre. Thus, the achievements of the workers, and the party that ruled in their name, were reinforced through the arts.

- Music suffered the most from emigrations abroad but the emergence of the classical composer **Shostakovich** showed that talent could survive within the system. At the popular end of the market jazz music made its first appearance in Russia, to mixed reviews.
- Radio and the cinema, as fairly recent developments, were easier for the Bolsheviks to influence. Neither had a long tradition of independent activity. Radio had broadcast news of the Revolution in October 1917 in Morse code. Soviet scientists quickly developed voice radio and by 1921 programmes were being broadcast. The *Spoken Newspaper of the Russian Telegraph Agency* featured news and propaganda material with little emphasis on music. Radio receivers were expensive and in order to get their message to the people the Bolsheviks installed loudspeakers in public places, factories and clubs. Control of radio communications was centralised through the Commissariat for Posts and Telegraph and, as the government recognised the importance of this form of communication, resources were given to ensure rapid development. By 1922 Moscow had the most powerful broadcasting station in the world.
- The other relatively new development was that of the cinema which was to have an important role in popular culture. Lenin had stated that 'the cinema is for us the most important of all the arts' and film was used to promote political messages. The work of directors such as **Sergei Eisenstein** and Alexander Dovzhenko was to put Soviet film-making at the forefront of world cinema. Eisenstein had already made *Strike* by 1924 and *Battleship Potemkin* was in production, to be released in 1925. His use of montage and imagery, as well as technical experimentation, made Eisenstein's work truly innovative but it was sometimes too sophisticated for the audience. Escapist American and German films were more popular in the early 1920s.
- In other areas of popular culture government control was extended. The State Publishing Organisation, **GOSIZDAT**, achieved a state monopoly over the press during the Civil War. The government also made use of festivals to develop a new culture based on socialist values. The use of anniversaries of events connected to

KEY PEOPLE

Mikhail Sholokhov (1905–84) Soviet writer whose novels realistically depict the lives of people in rural Russia. His best known work is *And Quiet Flows the Don* (1934), set during the Civil War.

Anna Akhmatova (1888–1966) Considered to be one of the greatest Russian poets. Her poems in the early 1920s often contained patriotic themes and demonstrated that high-quality work could still be produced under the Bolshevik regime.

Dmitri Shostakovich (1906–75) Composer of classical music. Although he did not produce his major works until after 1925, he trained in Petrograd between 1919–25 and showed that major talent could still be nurtured within Bolshevik Russia.

Sergei Eisenstein (1898–1948) Cinema film producer who was prepared to use his talents to support the Bolshevik regime. Worked for Moscow's Workers' Theatre before moving into the film industry. His first film *Strike* (1924) was about the oppression of the workers by the ruling classes. Later films included *October: Ten Days That Shook the World*, a dramatisation of the Revolution. Although much of his work was propaganda, Eisenstein was also able to produce films that were highly innovative and showed technical excellence.

the Revolution and May Day to honour the workers all helped instil and reinforce the values of the new state, even if extra food rations were sometimes used as an incentive for crowds to turn up.

By 1924 the Bolshevik Revolution had accelerated some of the trends evident in the arts before 1917. The greater freedom of expression and experimentation which many artists had wished for was only partly achieved. As the government sought to extend its influence and control, there was a drift of talented artists out of the country, which had a negative impact on the quality and quantity of

Bolshevik propaganda – an idealised image of the Bolshevik Revolution.

> ## Summary of themes presented through Soviet arts and popular culture
>
> ### Machines and technology
> - promoted by the Constructivists e.g. Tatlin, in the early 1920s
> - related to using technology to build a new future
> - glorified objects which represented the worker or peasant.
>
> ### Futurism
> - emphasis on exploring the possibilities of the future
> - attacked traditional assumptions of 'bourgeois' art
> - influenced visionary utopianism, e.g. using architecture to create a new society based on communal living.

'high' culture, although some work of high quality survived. Attempts were made to raise the status of popular culture and promote the values of the new regime, and the Constructivists were able to achieve some bridging of the gap between artist and worker which widened participation in the arts. The other trend in evidence was one of a more inward-looking culture, focusing on Soviet developments as well as those from the West. The Bolsheviks were starting to realise how new technologies could be harnessed to the arts and popular culture for the benefit of the government and it was this trend which was to dominate in the period after 1924.

SUMMARY QUESTIONS

1 How did the policies of the Bolshevik Party towards women and the family change between 1917 and 1924?

2 What attempts were made by the Bolsheviks to reduce the influence of religion between 1917 and 1924?

3 What impact did the Bolshevik regime have on the arts and popular culture between 1917 and 1924?

8: The struggle for power after Lenin's death, 1924–9: Safeguarding the Revolution?

Paralysed since 1922 by a series of strokes, Lenin died in January 1924. He was immediately accorded god-like status by the party and Petrograd was renamed Leningrad in his honour.

The period 1924 to 1929 was marked by a debate over the direction the Revolution should take. The situation which Lenin left behind was uncertain because Lenin himself had not given clear directions as to the path that should be followed. The Bolshevik regime in 1924 was unsure as to how the Revolution should be progressed. The NEP, although starting to yield economic results, was a source of much controversy. It was very much part of Lenin's legacy to the party but it was seen by most party members as a temporary phase. The issue of when and how to change the NEP became a central concern amongst the priorities that the party needed to set in order to ensure the Revolution was safeguarded. This debate over the future of the Revolution was to become tied to a power struggle between the leading Bolsheviks over who should succeed Lenin as leader of the Soviet Union.

THE RISE OF STALIN

From the collective leadership which was to rule the Soviet Union immediately after Lenin's death, Stalin was to emerge as the dominant figure, removing his colleagues and establishing his position as sole leader of the state. To most other members of the Communist Party in 1924 this development would have been viewed as unlikely because the majority of the party saw Trotsky as the most likely successor to Lenin. In the power struggle that developed it was Stalin, not Trotsky, who was able to outmanoeuvre the **Politburo** and secure the leadership.

Stalin and Trotsky: differences in personality

When comparing Stalin and Trotsky it is clear that they were very different personalities and this fact was to have a significant bearing on how they reacted to the circumstances that presented themselves after 1924.

Stalin's background provides some clues to his later actions. He was born in the southern state of Georgia, the son of a cobbler from peasant stock. His mother wanted him to become more than just a shoemaker and he was sent first to a church school and later to a theological seminary. But instead of learning religious ideas he became influenced by socialism and developed a deep sense of class hatred. 'Stalin', which meant 'man of steel', was an alias adopted by the young Joseph Djugashivili to help avoid detection by the Tsar's secret police as he undertook bank robberies to help finance the revolutionary movement. He was arrested six times between 1902 and 1913 for revolutionary activity. Stalin's efforts in the revolutionary cause had brought him to the attention of Lenin, who was impressed by his organising ability and willingness to obey orders. As early as 1912 Stalin had become one of the six members of the **Central Committee** of the Bolshevik Party and he had helped to set up the party's newspaper *Pravda*.

Lenin hoped Stalin would give the Central Committee more of a practical and proletarian image than the intellectuals who made up the majority of the party's leadership. As one of Lenin's most loyal followers Stalin was rewarded with the position of Commissar for Nationalities after the October Revolution. In this role, Stalin was involved in organising the Caucasus region during the Civil War, including some responsibility over military authority. This role brought him into conflict with Trotsky, who was in charge of the Red Army, and this seems to have been the start of their personal rivalry. Stalin's work in the Caucasus region also made Lenin aware of some of Stalin's faults. He had been rather heavy-handed in the dismissal of Georgian national representatives and Lenin was forced to intervene in order to resolve the situation. Thus, early in his career, Stalin had exhibited the leading features of his character: he was an able and shrewd administrator with a tendency to ruthlessness. Stalin was not an intellectual or Marxist theorist, indeed his grasp of ideology was limited, but he was driven by a sense of class hatred, stemming from his humble background and early life in Tsarist Russia.

Trotsky may have shared a tendency to authoritarianism with Stalin but in other respects they were completely different personalities. Trotsky had been a brilliant student. Born near Odessa, he studied mathematics at the town's university and it soon became obvious that he had a formidable intellect and was a superb orator. He was at his best when dealing with a crisis. His thorough and energetic preparation and execution of the October Revolution and his work in organising the Red Army during the Civil War showed these qualities at their best. But there was another side to Trotsky. He was a Jew by birth and his 'Jewishness' did lead to some prejudice against him in the party. His intellectual background made him arrogant and those party members and opponents who came into conflict with Trotsky often found themselves at the sharp end of his wit and sarcasm. His arrogance and indifference in party matters were to lead to a lack of judgement on occasions. Trotsky was not a team player and made little attempt to endear himself to others. His main qualities were, by his own admission, 'unsociability, individualism and aristocratism'. His attitude, that it was only he who held in his mind the larger picture of actions and their implications and let others concern themselves with details, did not go down well with his colleagues.

Trotsky had been a Menshevik until the summer of 1917 and his late conversion was seen as opportunism as well as a lack of commitment to the party. He rarely attended party meetings and his lack of support in the party was shown when he came tenth in elections to the Central Committee at the tenth Party Congress in 1921. Many Bolsheviks wondered whether Trotsky was a man of the party or was working to his own agenda. These concerns were to become more significant after 1917 with the Bolsheviks' obsession with the fate of their Revolution. An examination of the course of the earlier French Revolution showed the possible dangers. Out of the French Revolution Napoleon Bonaparte had emerged as dictator. Would the Bolshevik Revolution suffer the same fate? Many Bolsheviks were concerned that a potential Bonaparte could be lurking in the party and they assumed it would be a charismatic figure with grand visions and army connections. Trotsky's personality and background made him, in the minds of many Bolsheviks, the most likely candidate for this role and these suspicions generated a degree of hostility to Trotsky from within the party.

The differences in personality between Stalin and Trotsky were to be highlighted in the manner in which each individual adapted to and made use of the situation that arose in 1924 when Lenin died.

Joseph Stalin.

Personalities: Stalin and Trotsky

Joseph Stalin (1879–1953)
- from a peasant family background
- deep sense of class hatred
- practically-minded
- shrewd
- effective administrator
- ruthless and heavy-handed.

Leon Trotsky (1879–1940)
- from a wealthy, Jewish family background
- previously a Menshevik and his conversion to the Bolshevik cause was viewed by other Bolsheviks with suspicion
- formidable intellect
- appeared arrogant
- poor sense of judgement when dealing with other people
- unwilling to cultivate support within the Bolshevik Party
- preferred to work as an individual rather than as part of a team.

The situation in 1924

There was some confusion in 1924 because Lenin had given no clear indication of what the power structure should be after he had gone. This resulted in an uncertain atmosphere, which worked to Stalin's advantage. Even before Lenin's death Stalin had laid the basis of his power. He had become **General Secretary** of the Party in 1922 and used the powers and influence of this position to gather information. Even Lenin's private home was bugged in order to keep Stalin supplied with information. Whilst Lenin was recovering from his series of strokes at Gorky it was Stalin who provided the link between the leader and the Politburo. After his third stroke in March 1923 Lenin lost all powers of speech except monosyllables such as 'vot vot' (here, here). Stalin was thus in a very powerful position. Above all, he recognised that the main focus of power was not the government but the party's Politburo. The growth in the scope and responsibility of the state had made some positions more important than others and as the party had developed into the organs for administering the state it was the party structure which grew in power. The head of the party structure was the General Secretary and in 1924 it was Stalin who held this post.

Stalin's positions within the party

By 1924 Stalin had gained not only useful influence within the party but also invaluable experience of how it functioned. As Commissar for Nationalities, a post he held from 1917 until 1923, Stalin was in charge of the officials in the various republics outside Russia. In 1919 Stalin was also appointed as Liaison Officer between the Politburo and the Orgburo (the party's bureau of organisation), a post which allowed him to monitor party personnel and policy. In the same year Stalin was made Head of the Workers' and Peasants' Inspectorate, a wide-ranging post which involved the overseeing of the work of all government departments. The key position, however, was that of General Secretary of the party, which Stalin gained in 1922. This gave him access to over 26,000 personal files of party members – a useful source of information which could be used against rivals. In this post he had Dzerzhinsky, the head of the secret police, report to him regularly. There were few Politburo members not under his

KEY TERM

General Secretary This position was the head of the Party Secretariat, which was responsible for the day-to-day running of the party. The General Secretary co-ordinated work across all party departments and had access to a vast range of information which could be used to appoint local party officials. As the party organisation grew, so did the power and influence of the General Secretary.

surveillance. More importantly, the position of General Secretary gave Stalin the power of patronage. He had the right to appoint people to party positions and this provided him with a tool to promote his own supporters to key roles. As time went on, more and more party officials owed their loyalty to Stalin. As the 1920s progressed those who opposed Stalin were removed from the Politburo and replaced by Molotov, Kalinin and Voroshilov, all cronies of Stalin. Kirov was made head of the party in Leningrad in 1926 when Stalin wanted a loyal supporter to replace the out-of-favour Zinoviev. When it came to votes on party issues, Stalin could always out-vote and out-manoeuvre his opponents. The levers of power were in his hands. In contrast, Trotsky remained Commissar for War until 1925, a position which provided him with useful links with the army but less influence in the party structure as a whole. In fact, as Commissar for War Trotsky had been made responsible for the requisitioning of grain during the Civil War and this gained him little support amongst the rural population.

Stalin's positions in the party

- People's Commissar for Nationalities (1917)
- Liaison Officer between the Politburo and the Orgburo (1919)
- Head of the Workers' and Peasants' Inspectorate (1919)
- General Secretary of the Party (1922)

Stalin did not create the party structure but he was able to use it to his advantage. His capacity for thoroughness in administration could prosper in this set-up. He had gained the position of General Secretary because others had turned it down as being too uninteresting but it suited Stalin's skills and provided a useful cover for any ambitions he might have. Some party members nicknamed Stalin 'Comrade Card-Index', a reference to his willingness to undertake routine administrative tasks. Sukhanov referred to Stalin as the 'grey blur', a good administrator but someone who lacked personality. These comments may seem like criticisms of Stalin's qualities but in the circumstances of 1924 and with the party's fear of a Bonaparte figure emerging, these qualities were a positive advantage.

Structural changes in the party

Between 1923 and 1925 the party increased its membership by launching the '**Lenin Enrolment**' – a move designed to enhance Stalin's power. The aim of this membership drive was to increase the number of true proletarians in the party ranks. Over 500,000 workers were recruited, doubling the party's membership, and this was to have important consequences. The new members were largely poorly educated and politically naïve. They may have seen party membership as an opportunity to further their career and escape from the working class; certainly many of these new members made successful careers in the party structure. It is clear that these new members saw the party as a source of privileges and that retaining these privileges depended on loyalty to those who had allowed them into the party. As General Secretary, it was Stalin who was responsible for supervising the 'Lenin Enrolment' and it greatly extended his influence in the party. He could provide party officials with better living quarters, additional food rations and trips abroad to recuperate from illness. Stalin's humble background may well have helped him in the identification of the needs and demands of these new members and, in the power struggle which followed, he was careful to make his views echo those of the rank and file.

Lenin's funeral

One obvious opportunity which Stalin had for presenting himself to the party was at the funeral of Lenin, an occasion which demonstrated both the skills of Stalin in manipulating events and Trotsky's lack of judgement and tactical weaknesses. Although the Politburo had declared itself a collective leadership on the death of Lenin, manoeuvring behind the scenes was already evident. Stalin gained the advantage of being the one who delivered the oration at Lenin's funeral. This enabled him to present himself as the chief mourner and also gave him an opportunity to highlight his intention of continuing the

KEY TERM

Lenin Enrolment A campaign launched between 1923 and 1925 to increase the membership of the Bolshevik Party, particularly the number of industrial workers in the party.

Crowds at Lenin's funeral, 1924.

work of Lenin. In contrast, Trotsky did not even turn up at the funeral. The reasons for his absence are still unclear but the excuse he gave was that Stalin had not informed him of the date. This was a rather lame excuse and it comes across as rather unconvincing. Whatever the reasons for his absence, it was a serious tactical mistake as it raised doubts about Trotsky's respect for Lenin. Trotsky also missed an opportunity to undermine Stalin by his refusal, along with Zinoviev, to publish Lenin's Testament. This document set out Lenin's views on each member of the Politburo with suggestions on how they should be used in the future. Of Stalin, Lenin had written that he 'is too rude' and recommended his removal from the position of General Secretary. Unfortunately, Lenin was also critical of

---

Lenin's Testament

This was a document written by Lenin in December 1922; a postscript was added in January 1923. In it he set out his views on the way forward for the Bolshevik Revolution after his death. He used it to assess the strengths and weaknesses of each of the leading Bolsheviks and made comments on how they should be used in the future. Owing to its critical content the document was not released when Lenin died in 1924.

the other members of the Politburo and as a result the Testament was suppressed.

The 'Lenin legacy'

KEY CONCEPT

Lenin legacy A term used to describe the policies and ideas of Lenin after his death. Given the god-like status acquired by Lenin after 1924, it was seen as important and politically useful to protect the Revolution as it had been inherited from Lenin.

In the atmosphere of hero worship, which was prevalent at the funeral, Stalin was able to present himself as the heir to the '**Lenin legacy**'. Despite the objections of Krupskaya, Lenin's wife, it was decided to embalm Lenin's body. The decision may well have been Stalin's; if not, he certainly approved of it. Lenin quickly became an almost god-like figure to the party and Stalin, from his early experience in a theological seminary, was aware of the power of religious symbolism. To present oneself as the worthy successor of the Lenin legacy was to make a formidable bid for power. Stalin emphasised the need to apply the ideas of Lenin and this carried more weight from someone like Stalin, who seemed to have few ideas of his own. Stalin inaugurated the Lenin Institute to further the study of Lenin's works and gave a series of lectures on Leninism at the Communist University in Moscow. Trotsky, on the other hand, completely misjudged this mood and launched an attack on Lenin's New Economic Policy in his essays *Lessons on October* (1924).

Trotsky's attack on party bureaucracy

KEY PERSON

Grigory Zinoviev (1883–1936) A leading member of the left-wing of the party. Zinoviev was a volatile personality, subject to mood swings and he found Stalin difficult to deal with. Stalin used Zinoviev and Kamenev to form a triumvirate against Trotsky but after Trotsky's defeat Stalin turned against them. In 1926, Zinoviev joined the 'United Opposition' (with Trotsky and Kamenev) but was demoted from the Politburo and expelled from the party in 1927. After publicly admitting to mistakes and praising Stalin, Zinoviev was readmitted to the party before being expelled again in 1932. He was tried in a show trial in 1936 for crimes against the state and executed.

As well as attacking the policies of Lenin, Trotsky also criticised the growing bureaucracy in the party, which he saw as leading to a loss of the revolutionary spirit. These comments were to increase his unpopularity. To Trotsky the bureaucracy had grown to the point where it was in danger of becoming the master rather than the servant of the people. The bureaucracy had, of course, grown in number under Lenin and as such Trotsky's comments could again be seen as a criticism of Lenin's work. As the party was now the main vehicle for social mobility in the Soviet Union, its members were anxious to protect their privileges. Trotsky's attack on party bureaucracy was therefore seen as a threat and as a result there was little support for him within the party. When these criticisms came to a head in early 1924, Trotsky faced opposition from a triumvirate of Stalin, **Zinoviev** and **Kamenev**. Trotsky's support was confined to a few cells in the party, the universities and the Red Army. The triumvirate, on the other hand, could mobilise most of the party apparatus in its favour due to Stalin's influence as General Secretary. When delegates to the Thirteenth Party Conference were elected in 1924 Trotsky's supporters were small in number. Trotsky made little attempt to organise himself and his supporters within the party. He felt that inter-party squabbling was beneath him and his arrogance again became a problem. He made few efforts to win friends. Stalin's tactics were able to reap more rewards. The mobilisation of support in the party through his influence as General Secretary was one tactic which he was to repeat later on several occasions when faced with opposition. One factor in his favour was Lenin's rule against factionalism, **'On Party Unity'**. This had been issued in the aftermath of the Kronstadt Mutiny of 1921 when the party had faced serious opposition. It condemned the forming of factions in the party and may well have limited Trotsky's attempts to organise his supporters; he would have been aware that the accusation of factionalism was a serious charge which carried the death penalty. Stalin could always use the accusation of factionalism to frustrate opposition within the party. It was a weapon he was to use to good effect against his opponents when differences arose over ideology and policy.

In 1926 Stalin was in a position to deal effectively with Trotsky. The levers of power were in Stalin's hands and he was able to mobilise his support in the party to defeat Trotsky and his supporters. By 1929 not only was Trotsky no longer in the party, he was no longer in the Soviet Union, expelled on Stalin's orders. Stalin had shown himself to be highly skilled in manipulating the situation after 1924. His personality was better suited to political manoeuvring than that of Trotsky but ultimately it was Stalin's position within the party structures and the manner in which he aligned himself with the attitudes of party members that sealed his victory. To the rank and file membership Stalin represented a safer future for them and the Revolution than the more 'dangerous' figure of Trotsky. It was perhaps not just Stalin who was successful but the system itself.

United Opposition The
alliance formed in 1926 by
those on the left of the party:
Trotsky, Zinoviev and
Kamenev. The United
Opposition was formed to
oppose the continuation of
the NEP. As Trotsky had
been a former enemy of
Zinoviev and Kamenev it was
a strange alliance that lacked
conviction. By this time all
three leaders of the 'United
Opposition' were seen as
outsiders and Stalin was able
to use the party machinery to
defeat them. Accused of
factionalism they were
expelled from the party.

KEY PERSON

**Nikolai Bukharin
(1888–1938)** A leading
economic theorist who was
very much on the left of the
party until the NEP. He
became strongly opposed to
the forced industrialisation of
the Soviet Union and was one
of the most vocal in support
of the continuation of the
NEP. When Stalin became
convinced that the NEP must
go Bukharin's position was
under threat. Bukharin
refused to build up a power
base in the party due to a
sense of loyalty and as a result
he was in a weak position. He
was removed from the
Politburo in 1929 but
continued to support the
Right Opposition. He was
executed during the purges of
1938.

DIVISIONS OVER THE FUTURE OF THE REVOLUTION

The events, which saw the defeat not just of Trotsky and the Left but also of the Right of the party leadership, were centred on debates and divisions over the best way forward for the Revolution. The role of Stalin in these debates does, in itself, illustrate his tactics of manoeuvring himself into a dominant position whilst outmanoeuvring and isolating his opponents.

The defeat of the Left

All of the Bolshevik leaders were committed to the building of socialism in the Soviet Union and saw that industrialisation and urbanisation were the keys to achieving this. On this they were all agreed. The differences arose over the methods and speed of this development and the division between the Left and the Right of the Communist Party was centred around a difference of emphasis on two main issues; the future of the NEP and the call for 'Permanent Revolution'.

The future of the NEP. This was an issue which quickly came to the fore after Lenin's death. Lenin himself had viewed the NEP as a temporary measure needed to get the economy going again after the privations of the Civil War and to win over the peasantry to the Bolshevik Revolution. However, Lenin had given little indication of how long this temporary phase should last. The Left saw the NEP, with its emphasis on elements of capitalist free enterprise, as a betrayal of the aims of the Revolution. The compromise with the peasantry, allowing them the right to sell surpluses at market for a profit, was seen as holding back the move towards a true proletarian state based on socialist principles. The Right, on the other hand, saw the NEP as a legitimate policy which should be retained as long as it worked; in other words, so long as the nation's food needs were met.

In this debate Trotsky, Zinoviev and Kamenev put forward the views of the Left, forming the so-called '**United Opposition**' in 1926. The Right was led by **Bukharin**, **Rykov** and **Tomsky**. The differences between Left and

Right were outlined in debates between the economist **Preobrazhensky**, a supporter of the United Opposition, and Bukharin from the Right. Preobrazhensky, from the viewpoint of an economist, argued that resources such as food would have to be extracted from the peasantry to support any industrialisation. Bukharin, from a political viewpoint, saw the importance of the alliance between the workers and peasants, which Lenin's NEP had created, in ensuring the survival of the regime. Where did Stalin stand in this debate? The fact that he did not participate in the debate led most to conclude that he supported his old ally Bukharin.

The call for 'Permanent Revolution'. The ideological debate also became tied to a questioning of loyalty through the issue of 'Permanent Revolution' put forward by Trotsky. The priority, according to Trotsky, was the need to spread worldwide revolution to secure the success of the Bolshevik takeover in Russia. Without this revolutionary zeal the party would succumb to conservative forces and the bureaucracy would lose sight of its original role of working on behalf of the proletariat and operate in its own interests. The idea of Permanent Revolution was to cause division in 1925 when Stalin was to make his mark on policy direction by promoting the idea of 'Socialism in One Country'. It was already clear that the wave of world revolution that the Bolsheviks had hoped for after 1917 had failed to materialise. Communist uprisings in Germany, Hungary and even in Glasgow had all failed. The Soviet Union was on her own, surrounded by hostile states. Stalin's slogan of 'Socialism in One Country' was a recognition of this reality. It called for modernisation through industrialisation by utilising the resources of the Soviet Union. To many of the old Bolsheviks this was disturbing as it ignored a major aspect of traditional Marxist theory: the need for a revolution on a world scale to bring down capitalism. The focus of 'Socialism in One Country' was on the Soviet Union and had undertones of nationalism and patriotism. Trotsky was thus provoked into an attack on Stalin's policy, which enabled Stalin to present himself as a true patriot. How could the Soviet Union survive in a hostile world unless it first strengthened its position by industrialisation? Promoting world

Alexei Rykov (1881–1938) Became Head of the Government on the death of Lenin and was an ally of Stalin against Trotsky. A leading member of the Right in the party over the issue of the NEP: Rykov was strongly in favour of its retention. When Stalin decided to end the NEP Rykov's position was threatened. He was dismissed as Head of the Government by Stalin in 1930, arrested in 1937 for allegedly planning to assassinate Stalin and executed in 1938.

Evgeny Preobrazhensky (1886–1937) The leading economic theorist of the party in the 1920s. He was firmly on the left of the party and sided with Trotsky over the NEP. Preobrazhensky urged the immediate abandonment of the NEP and the introduction of a socialist economy. He was expelled from the party in 1927 but with Trotsky also out of the way by 1927 Stalin felt able to steal Preobrazhensky's ideas. He was arrested, tried and executed in 1937.

Mikhail Tomsky (1880–1936) A trade unionist who was on the right of the party. He supported Bukharin in the debate over the NEP and as a result fell out with Stalin in 1930. He was removed from the Politburo but continued to fight for trade union rights. Due to be put on trial with Bukharin and Rykov, he committed suicide in 1936.

'Permanent Revolution' versus 'Socialism in One Country'

Permanent Revolution The name of the policy vigorously promoted by Trotsky, which saw the need to spread world revolution as the priority after the Bolshevik Revolution of 1917. Trotsky argued that without world revolution the Revolution in Russia would not survive.

Socialism in One Country The name given to the policy promoted by Stalin in the 1920s, which saw the strengthening of the Revolution within Russia as more important than spreading revolution abroad.

revolution, Stalin argued, could only be achieved after the Soviet Union was on a secure footing; to do otherwise was seen as irresponsible.

The formation of the United Opposition in 1926 gave Trotsky a focus for organising his position. Yet his alliance with Zinoviev and Kamenev was an uneasy and unconvincing one due to their past disagreements and they made little attempt to organise mass support for the Left's argument. Stalin was therefore able to overcome the United Opposition by exploiting their divisions and using his power as General Secretary to deliver the votes needed to defeat them. Although the United Opposition were able to present their arguments at a Central Committee meeting in 1926, they were defeated and at the Fifteenth Party Conference, later in the same year, they were not allowed to speak. From this point onwards the Opposition had to work in secret and, accused of forming factions, they were expelled from the Politburo and either demoted or sent into internal exile. Zinoviev and Kamenev were allowed to stay in the party after renouncing their previous views but Trotsky preferred to stick to his principles and was exiled to Alma-Ata in Central Asia.

The defeat of the Right

The defeat of the Left Opposition raised the political temperature and in the winter of 1927–8 the party leadership found itself once again divided over the issue of industrialisation as Stalin aimed to launch the First Five Year Plan to galvanise the economy. Rather than a deep ideological division, the disagreement was over when and how industrialisation should take place. All of the Bolshevik leadership saw industrialisation as a necessary part of the consolidation of socialism and with it the Communist Party itself but divisions occurred over the role of the peasantry in this. In the absence of foreign capital how could the Soviet Union raise the resources needed to support large-scale industrialisation? The peasants would have to produce the food surpluses needed to support the growth in industry and with it the growth of towns. The Left saw force as the only way to do this whereas the Right preferred a policy of persuasion, arguing that the use of force could actually cause food production to decline because of opposition from the peasantry. In early 1928, within months of the defeat of the Left, the proposals for the Five Year Plan led to the emergence of a **Right Opposition** group, which began to argue the case of the Right for a continuation of the framework introduced by the NEP and that any economic targets be kept low so as to avoid the need for force to ensure that they were met. The leaders of the Right in the Politburo were Tomsky, the trade union leader, Rykov, who was the official head of the Soviet Government, and Bukharin, the editor of the communist newspaper *Pravda* and a distinguished economic theorist.

KEY TERM

The Right Opposition
Those in the party who wished to see the continuation of the NEP, rather than Stalin's forced industrialisation of the USSR under the first Five Year Plan. Its leaders were Bukharin, Rykov and Tomsky. By 1930 they had been removed from their positions of power in the party. The Right Opposition was finally dealt with in the purges in 1938: most of its members were executed.

In this debate Stalin saw the views of the Right as standing in the way of his policy of 'Socialism in One Country', threatening to slow down any progress that could be made in strengthening the economic base of the Soviet Union and socialism. After the removal of the threat from the Left it seemed that Stalin was prepared to adopt their ideas of rapid industrialisation by abandoning the NEP.

Why did Stalin suddenly become convinced that the only way forward was to impose industrialisation on the country?

In 1927 there was a great deal of anxiety over an impending attack by the capitalist powers during which the peasants started to hoard their produce and shortages occurred in the industrial towns. It became clear to Stalin that the peasants were a major factor in holding back the industrial development of the Soviet Union. Without an increase in food production further industrialisation could not be supported. He was also aware of a growing disillusionment among the party rank and file over the course of the Revolution. The Nepmen, kulaks and 'bourgeois experts' who had survived due to the compromises of the NEP were the target of their frustration. This dissatisfaction was building up in the party and Stalin saw the potential of aligning himself with these views in order to strengthen his own position. Rapid industrialisation would provide an opportunity to sweep away the remnants of the old system and move to socialism. Thus, Stalin was reacting to trends and attitudes within the party and differences in ideology provided an opportunity to defeat the Right.

The position of the Right was weakened by Bukharin's refusal to try to build up an organised faction within the Party. He was, no doubt, aware of the penalties associated with faction building that had been used against Trotsky. Bukharin's sense of loyalty meant that this debate was carried out behind closed doors and there was no direct appeal to the party members for support. The Right's power was based around the Moscow party organisation, led by Uglanov, and the Central Council of Trade Unions, led by the Politburo member, Tomsky. Both Uglanov and Tomsky were removed from their positions in the autumn of 1928. By early 1929 the Right Opposition in the Politburo was identified by name and all were removed from their posts except Rykov, who remained Head of the Government until 1930.

By 1929 both the Left and the Right of the party had been defeated by Stalin. In this struggle for power Stalin had made effective use of the party organisation and structures. The fact that party divisions were based around debates over the future of the Revolution were to have important consequences. As the collective leadership which had been declared in 1924 at the death of Lenin was whittled away, Stalin was gaining the power necessary to ensure that his own view on how the Revolution should progress could be implemented. He was now in a position to launch the Five Year Plans unhindered. To Stalin and his supporters these were the policies essential to the survival of the Revolution; to his opponents they were to mark a betrayal of Lenin's Revolution.

SUMMARY QUESTIONS

1 How did Stalin use his position as General Secretary, before 1924, to increase his power and influence?

2 How and why did Stalin try to identify himself with the 'Lenin legacy'?

3 How did the Right and Left of the Bolshevik Party disagree in the period 1924–8 over the future path the Revolution should take?

4 Why was Stalin able to defeat both the Left and Right of the party by 1929?

9: Soviet foreign policy, 1917-28: Safeguarding the Revolution?

On initial study, Soviet foreign policy from 1917 to 1928 can seem confused and contradictory both in its aims and its methods. It was aiming to protect the new state from hostile neighbours and to ensure its very survival, yet at the same time trying to promote the spread of world revolution through **Comintern** (a Communist-controlled organisation). This latter aim, however, tended to provoke foreign governments even more. After 1920, the first of these two aims was to take precedence but the activities of the Comintern continued. The methods used to pursue foreign policy aims were also confused and sometimes contradictory as the growing tension in international relations caused the government to constantly reassess its tactics. The Soviet Union had, since 1917, been working from a position of weakness and its manoeuvring needs to be seen in this context. By 1928 it had little to show for its foreign policy efforts. Yet the lack of tangible results was not always of the government's own making and, despite policy failures, the Soviet Union had survived in a hostile world.

KEY TERM

Comintern An organisation set up in 1919 to facilitate contacts between communist groups throughout the world. The Soviet government was able to control its activities. It was dissolved in 1943.

Aims

Two aims can be identified in Soviet foreign policy:

- To ensure the survival of the new Communist State against hostile neighbours
- To spread world revolution.

In the optimism of the period immediately after the Bolshevik Revolution of 1917, it was the second aim which was to the fore. World revolution, as predicted by Marx, was to be encouraged by the Third International, known as Comintern, an organisation set up by the Bolsheviks to co-ordinate communist groups throughout the world. The Bolsheviks hoped, even if they did not believe, that the capitalist West would soon collapse and that this would render traditional foreign relations pointless. To some Bolsheviks this aim would be crucial to the survival of the regime. Trotsky was to state: 'Either the Russian Revolution will create a revolutionary movement in Europe, or the European powers will destroy the Russian Revolution.'

As the prospects for world revolution faded the Soviet Union's foreign policy became much more concerned with ensuring the survival of the new regime. Surrounded by potentially hostile nations, to whom communism represented a threat to both their political and economic systems, the Soviet government began to adopt more traditional aims. Lenin was to take a more realistic view of the world situation than Trotsky and the replacement of Trotsky by **Chicherin** as Commissar for Foreign Affairs in 1918 emphasised this trend towards a more traditional view of the interests of the state.

KEY PEOPLE

Georgy Chicherin (1872–1936) Commissar for Foreign Affairs between 1918 and 1930. Chicherin was of noble birth and gave the Bolsheviks an air of respectability in foreign affairs. He had traditional views towards foreign policy and used it to represent the interests of the state.

Georgy Chicherin.

Trotsky and foreign affairs

Trotsky believed that the Russian Revolution would only survive if the rest of Europe also fell to the revolutionary movement. If Europe remained predominantly capitalist the Russian Revolution would be swept away by an invasion of the Western capitalist powers. To prevent this happening Trotsky believed that it was essential to aid the spread of the revolutionary movement to other countries.

Vyacheslav Molotov (1890–1986) Became Head of the Comintern in 1926 and Commissar for Foreign Affairs in 1939. He used foreign affairs as an opportunity to upset other countries and, to the West, he represented the unattractive side of Bolshevik Russia. Molotov was a skilled politician and was able to retain Stalin's favour throughout his career. Thus, despite being one of Stalin's cronies he was a great survivor.

Internal Soviet politics were also to have an influence on foreign policy. After 1926 foreign relations became influenced by Stalin's concern to pursue 'Socialism in One Country' and the emphasis on world revolution was lessened still further. In this year Zinoviev was replaced as head of Comintern by Bukharin and in 1929 internal political rivalry led to Bukharin's replacement by **Molotov**, one of Stalin's cronies. The bringing of Comintern under Stalin's centralised control was a sign that the more traditional aims of the Commissariat for Foreign Affairs had gained the upper hand, yet, despite this priority, the Communist Party never completely abandoned the aim of world revolution.

METHODS

In pursuing its foreign policy aims the Soviet government adopted a range of methods which were often muddled and inconsistent. This was in itself a reflection of the weakness of the international position the Soviet Union found itself in; ready to latch onto any policy that suited its purposes. Thus, collective security through the League of Nations was condemned when the USSR stood outside it but supported when the government thought it might bring results. The Bolsheviks claimed that peace and disarmament were the guiding principles of their foreign policy but war was also pursued. In this respect, despite the claims that Soviet foreign policy was uniquely progressive and therefore markedly different to that of the imperialistic powers, propaganda was a key weapon in foreign policy. Propaganda was to become a useful tool in justifying the shifts in policy which were to be taken between 1917 and 1928.

Deliberate provocation

On coming to power in 1917 the Bolsheviks were deliberately provocative in their foreign policy statements and actions. Stating a commitment to **open diplomacy**, the secret treaties signed by the Tsars were published and renounced. It was made quite clear to the West that commitments made by the Tsar to the Allies in the First World War would not be upheld. There was a real optimism amongst the Bolshevik leaders that revolution would spread and this led to the delaying tactics and bullish attitude adopted by the Soviet delegation which was negotiating the Treaty of Brest-Litovsk with Germany. If, as many Bolsheviks believed, Germany would soon collapse under the strain of class conflict caused by the war then the treaty was a rather pointless exercise. The Germans soon lost patience with this attitude and the treaty was forced on the Soviet government in March 1918, resulting in the loss of large areas of land (see map, p. 41). Finland, the Baltic States and Bessarabia were not regained when the treaty was annulled in 1919 after Germany's eventual defeat.

For a while it must have seemed as though the Comintern's hope of a world revolution was likely to bear fruit. There were communist uprisings in Hungary, where Bela Kun briefly established a communist government in 1920, and Germany, where there was both the Spartakist uprising in Berlin and a short-lived Soviet republic in Bavaria. Yet by the end of 1920 these hopes of a world revolution had been crushed. All of the communist uprisings in Europe had been dealt with and the USSR, after the devastation of the Civil War, found itself economically and militarily weak and surrounded by hostile states.

The War against Poland, 1920

The relative weakness of the new Soviet state was reinforced by the failure of Russia to defeat Poland in

KEY TERM

Open diplomacy One of the main criticisms the Bolsheviks had made of traditional foreign policy was that it was often conducted in secret. In reaction to this the Bolsheviks had made public all secret treaties signed by the Tsar. The Bolsheviks promised 'open diplomacy', a policy of greater openness in foreign affairs where diplomacy would be open to public scrutiny.

1920. The state of Poland was recreated under the Paris Peace Settlement of 1919, after the First World War. Under the settlement Poland was to receive land from Russia up to a line known as the Curzon Line. The new Polish leadership was unhappy with this arrangement, preferring to see Poland returned to its historic borders, and took the opportunity presented by the chaos of the Civil War in Russia to launch an attack on the new Bolshevik state. After early Bolshevik advances the Poles won a decisive victory outside Warsaw, the Polish capital. From this point onwards the Bolsheviks were in retreat and in October 1920 a ceasefire was signed. At the subsequent Treaty of Riga in 1921, the Bolsheviks handed over territory east of the Curzon Line, including parts of White Russia, to Poland. Lenin stated 'a bad peace was cheaper than a prolongation of war'. The war reinforced Lenin's awareness of Russia's vulnerability in a hostile world.

Accepting co-existence with the capitalist powers

Excluded from the Paris Peace Conference after the First World War and not invited to join the League of Nations, the USSR feared isolation in the international arena and this resulted in a change of emphasis. The USSR would have to come to terms with this situation and accept **co-existence** with the capitalist powers. Chicherin was instructed by Lenin to seek formal recognition for the Soviet Union and to stabilise its position in international affairs.

From 1921 onwards the Bolsheviks tried to develop relations with other countries to reduce their isolation and, as Lenin recognised, obtain foreign aid from various trade agreements. As the Bolsheviks had seized foreign assets in Russia without compensation this was not an easy task. Both Britain and France remained hostile to any agreement with a communist state, but Germany, as the other outcast in international relations, provided a more willing partner. The Genoa Conference, called by the Allies in 1922, provided the opportunity for Germany and the Soviet government to finalise the secret Treaty of Rapallo. This agreement resulted in secret diplomatic, military and economic links between the two countries. The USSR had quickly dropped its emphasis on open diplomacy. The

---

Relations with Germany

Both Germany and the USSR were outcasts from international affairs after the First World War and this drew them together. They signed the following agreements in the 1920s:

- The Rapallo Treaty, 1922
- The Treaty of Berlin, 1926.

Both treaties set up diplomatic, military and economic links between the two countries. The success of these links was, however, undermined by the activities of the Comintern.

---

results of the Rapallo Treaty for the USSR were limited by the Locarno Treaty of 1925 as Germany drew closer to Britain and France. The Treaty of Berlin of 1926 did, however, reaffirm the Rapallo agreement but the activities of Comintern in trying to stir up workers' revolution in Germany did not help relations.

Relations with Britain were improved in 1924 when the new Labour government of Ramsay MacDonald officially recognised the Soviet Union and a trade agreement, which had been signed in 1921, was extended. This improved relationship was short-lived when the Zinoviev letter became a major election issue later in the year. The letter, which was later revealed to be a forgery, incited the British workers to revolution. The incoming Conservative government was to break off formal relations with the Soviet Union once again in 1927. Formal relations were, however, established with Italy, France and Japan and by the end of the 1920s the position of the USSR in European affairs had improved. It was in the Far East that the USSR was suffering setbacks.

In China the Soviet government had supported the Chinese Nationalists (Kuomintang), which had been a broadly based party including the Chinese communists but this policy had suffered a serious setback in 1927 when the new leader of the Kuomintang, Chiang Kai-shek, launched

ТОВ. Ленин ОЧИЩАЕТ
ЗЕМЛЮ ОТ НЕЧИСТИ.

A Soviet cartoon showing Lenin sweeping away the world's capitalists and imperialists.

a vicious purge of the communist elements within his party. The so-called White Terror resulted in the massacre of communists in Shanghai and the remnants of the Chinese Communist Party were driven out of the main cities into the countryside. Yet more worrying for the USSR were the intentions of Japan in China, especially with regards to the Chinese province of Manchuria. Not only did the USSR have concessions in Manchuria but it also bordered the Soviet Union. The lack of firm direction in dealing with Japan made Stalin suspicious of Western policy. In this situation the USSR had to be very flexible in order to protect its interests.

RESULTS

If judged against its aims, Soviet foreign policy between 1917 and 1928 achieved only limited success. The aim of spreading world revolution had failed and became only a secondary concern after 1920. In terms of ensuring the survival of the Soviet Union against attack there was some success but it was to be short-term. The Soviet Union had struggled to reach any meaningful relationship with either Germany or Britain and France, yet this failure was hardly the fault of the USSR alone. All three countries were suspicious of the Soviet Union and were reluctant to enter wholeheartedly into any agreement with the new communist state.

The manoeuvring which Soviet policy underwent in this period was the result of the weak position the USSR found itself in. In the 1920s the chaos caused by the Civil War, after the First World War, greatly weakened the capacity of the USSR to influence international affairs. Despite Soviet weakness there were some achievements. The secret military links with Germany under the Rapallo Treaty had been valuable and went some way towards ending Soviet isolation. Yet the overall picture is one of confused and contradictory policies, with the USSR reacting to events rather than being able to influence them. The failures of foreign policy in this period thus showed that in order to affect world affairs the USSR had to be both economically and militarily strong.

SUMMARY QUESTIONS

1 What were the two principal aims of Bolshevik foreign policy between 1917 and 1928?

2 What were the consequences of the War with Poland for Soviet foreign policy?

3 How successful were the Bolsheviks in establishing friendly relations with foreign powers during this period?

AS ASSESSMENT: RUSSIA IN REVOLUTION, 1905–17

Using historical sources

Comprehension of sources

When considering historical sources it is necessary to bear in mind four key questions:

1 **Who?** Who is the author of the source? Is it a historian (and from which school of thought), a politician, a factory owner or a trade unionist? The background of the author may affect the style and content of the source. It is important to consider the values and attitudes of the author as these may be reflected in the source.
2 **What?** What does the source tell us? What is the content of the source? Does it ignore or neglect certain aspects? What it does not say can also be important. It is always worth thinking about the overall message. The rest of the content may well be the development of one basic point. It is also useful to consider the style, language and tone of the source as this often helps you to 'read between the lines' of what is being stated.
3 **When?** When was the source produced? Accounts produced at the time of the event have the advantage of immediacy; accounts written later have the advantage of hindsight. The fact that an author was an eyewitness could give a source considerable value.
4 **Why?** Why was the source produced? What is its purpose? Is it propaganda? What is the motive of the author?

By considering these four basic questions you are likely to be able to address wider issues about the usefulness, reliability and value of the sources you are studying. This will enable you comprehend the source in full.

Many questions involving sources will revolve around these aspects. Some questions may test your skills of comprehension by asking you to explain words or phrases in the context of the source. Other questions could ask you to explain the content and message of the source in a more developed manner; this type of question will require close reference to the source. This technique usually involves direct quotation of short phrases to support points you make. Comments such as 'see lines 8–20' are most unlikely to gain credit as they lack precision.

Remember that source-based questions are designed to test your skills in understanding and using sources as a historian and this is what you need to show in your answer.

Examples of sources and questions in the style of EDEXCEL

Source A: Letters from Alexandra to Nicholas II

20 Sept 1915
[Rasputin] begs you earnestly to name Protopopov there (Ministry of the Interior). You know him and had such a good impression of him – happens to be of the Duma [is not left] and so will know how to be with them.

27 Sept 1915
God bless your new choice of Protopopov – our Friend says you have done a very wise act in naming him.

28 Nov 1915
Now, before I forget, I must give you over a message from our Friend, prompted by what He saw in the night. He begs you to order that one should advance near Riga, says it is necessary, otherwise the Germans will settle down so firmly through all the winter, that it will cost endless bloodshed and trouble to make them move.

17 June 1916
[Rasputin] begs we should not yet strongly advance in the north because he says, if our successes continue being good in the south, they will themselves retreat from the north.

24 Nov 1916
I entreat you don't go and change Protopopov now, he will be alright, give him the chance to get the food supply matter into his hands and I assure you, all will go well. Of course I more than regret that Trepov (Minister of Transport) is at the head. Protopopov venerates our Friend and will be blessed. Don't change Protopopov.

6 Dec 1916
Once you have said that you want to keep Protopopov, how does he [Trepov, now Prime Minister] go against you? Bring down your fist on the table. Don't yield. Be the boss. Obey your firm little wife and our Friend. Believe in us.

From F. A. Golder, *Documents of Russian History 1914–17* (1964).

Source B: A police report on an incident in 1915
On 26 March of this year at about 11 p.m. the well-known Grigory Rasputin arrived at the Yar restaurant in the company of Anisia Reshetnikova, who is the

widow of a man of a respected family, an associate of the Moscow and Petrograd newspapers, Nikolai Soedov, and an unidentified young woman. The entire party was already in high spirits. Drunk, Rasputin danced the russkaya and then began confiding with the singers this type of thing: 'This caftan was a gift to me from the 'old lady' (Empress Alexandra), she sewed it, too.' Further, Rasputin's behaviour became truly outrageous, sexually psychopathic: he bared his sexual organs and in that state carried out a conversation with the singers, giving to some handwritten notes.

From Edvard Radzinsky *The Last Tsar: the life and death of Nicholas II* (1992).

Questions

> 1 Study Source A. Explain the meaning of 'Duma' (line 4) in the context of Source A.

Examiner's comments: This question is testing your understanding of a specific term. Examiners would be looking for a brief explanation of 'Duma' as the Russian parliament and for developing this by reference to the Tsar's use of the Duma and its role in government.

> 2 Study Source A. To what extent does Source A show Nicholas II to be a weak ruler?

Examiner's comments: This question is designed to let you show your skill in using a source as evidence. Answers would be expected to make close reference to the source. For higher marks, a consideration of 'to what extent' would be needed with a reasoned judgement on the source's value. On face value there is plenty of evidence in Source A to support the statement. The instruction he is given by Alexandra, 'Don't yield', indicates he was being pressured by other advisors and was likely to give in unless pushed by wife. Does the source prove Nicholas did what he was told to do by Alexandra and Rasputin? Not in itself. There could have been many other compelling reasons for appointing Protopopov.

> 3 Study Sources A and B. Assess the value of these sources to an historian studying the impact of Rasputin on the government.

Examiner's comments: This question is asking you to evaluate the sources as evidence of the impact of Rasputin on the government. Answers will be expected to provide a balance of comments on *both* sources. Higher level answers will consider the limitations as well as value of the sources to provide a fully rounded assessment.

Source A has value because it is taken from private letters in which Alexandra could express her views without regard for public sentiment. Her position in the government, especially during the war years, make this a valuable source. Yet the source is limited because it does not prove conclusively that Nicholas acted on her advice.

Source B would appear to have value because it comes from a police report compiled by officers who witnessed the incident with Rasputin. The language does, however, suggest a critical tone. One wonders what purpose the report was designed to serve. It may have been used as evidence by the police and government ministers, who disliked Rasputin, to undermine him and it could be deliberately exaggerated in order to shock the public. Thus, the source has limitations.

4 Study Sources A and B and use your own knowledge. Explain why support for the Tsarist regime collapsed between 1914 and 1917.

Examiner's comments: This question is designed to assess your ability to reach a judgement based on your analysis of sources and own knowledge.

Source A can be used to illustrate the weak character of Nicholas and the influence of both Alexandra and Rasputin on the government. These points could be developed by reference to your own knowledge, e.g. Rasputin's influence over Alexandra because of his apparent ability to control the pain of Alexis, the heir to the Russian throne, who suffered from haemophilia. Through Alexandra, Rasputin could exert an influence over Nicholas. The result of this was government chaos.

Source B develops the point about Rasputin by highlighting his scandalous behaviour. Your own knowledge could be used to develop this further by reference to the demoralising impact of scandals on the royal court.

Other factors from own knowledge could include: the impact of the First World War on the armed forces, the economic and social conditions in the towns and cities; the rise of revolutionary groups; and the increasing unrest in Petrograd. High level answers would be expected to assess the role of the First World War in speeding up long-term weaknesses in the Tsarist system, and to assess the relative importance of pressures from below (the revolutionaries), compared with the collapse at the top (the Tsar's own actions), and how the two were interlinked.

The consolidation of Bolshevik power: Russia 1918–29

Essay skills

Deconstructing essay questions

As a history student you are required to produce extended answers in the form of essays. At AS Level these will be structured essays, often broken down into two parts. These questions are designed to test your ability to understand historical issues and use information to support your views in the form of an argument.

When tutors ask you to write an essay, it is worth remembering that this is the standard way of getting you to show your historical understanding and ability to present an argument. Essay-writing is rather like producing a report in that it is essential to organise material into a logical sequence. In order to ensure that this is done effectively it is important to be aware of the demands of the question. You ignore the question at your peril!

How to deconstruct a question.
Break the question down into its constituent parts. Look for the following:

a) The **instruction** (I) e.g. 'examine', 'assess'.
b) The **topic** (T) e.g. Lenin's government, the October Revolution.
c) **Keywords** (KW) which need to be focused on in your answer.

EXAMPLE:
What impact did foreign intervention have on the Russian Civil War?

I – 'What'
T – Foreign intervention during the Russian Civil War
KW – 'impact', 'foreign intervention'.

If you spend some time thinking about the question and planning your answer you will save time later. This will also ensure that time is not wasted writing an inappropriate and irrelevant essay. A useful approach for planning is to deconstruct questions.

One of the most common reasons for underperforming in exams is the failure to produce a relevant answer. By using this process you will be able to plan your essays to ensure that the specific question asked is directly addressed.

Types of structured essay questions in the style of EDEXCEL

Essay questions can be divided into various categories depending on the instruction given. It is useful to think about the demands of each type of question.

1 Cause/effect questions. These questions usually start with 'why' or 'what' e.g. 'What factors led to the Bolshevik victory in the Civil War?' For this type of question, a list of factors provides a useful starting point but there is the danger that each factor is described rather than assessed. Think about dividing the factors into those which are either strengths of the Bolsheviks or weaknesses of the Whites. It is also essential to assess the relative importance of each factor. This will help you to develop an argument rather than just describe a list of factors involved.

2 Discussion questions. These quite often appear as a statement followed by the word 'discuss' or the phrase 'Do you agree?' e.g. '"We won the Civil War because the masses supported us" (Red Army Commander, 1921) How far do you agree with this explanation of Bolshevik victory in the Civil War?' The best way of dealing with this sort of question is to consider the evidence both for and against the statement given.

3 Significance/importance questions. These questions often start with phrases such as 'assess', 'how far' or 'to what extent'; instructions which require you to weigh up the significance/importance of a given factor. Example: 'Assess the contribution of Lenin to the consolidation of the Bolshevik regime in the period 1917–24'. These questions often look more specific than they actually are. For example, in order to assess the importance of Lenin in the consolidation of Bolshevik rule his role has to be compared with other individuals/factors.

4 Compare/contrast questions. These questions can be notoriously difficult for students. The key point to remember here is to ensure that the instruction is obeyed. For example, if asked to compare and contrast the roles of Lenin and Trotsky in the consolidation of Bolshevik rule it is quite common for students to describe the actions of each individual in turn with no real comparison until the conclusion. It is much better to think of headings under which they can be directly compared and contrasted, e.g. ideas, position, strengths and weaknesses, roles in the Revolution, roles in the Civil War etc.

Questions

1 Why did the Bolshevik government replace War Communism with the NEP?

Examiner's comments: This question requires knowledge of the reasons for the change in economic policy, e.g. the collapse of industrial production due to the Civil War, the unpopularity of War Communism, the Tambov Revolt and the Kronstadt Mutiny. Better answers will provide detailed information and show an ability to comment on the importance of each factor. The highest level will be for those answers that develop an overall argument supported by precise, detailed material.

2 To what extent had the NEP achieved its aims by 1928?

Examiner's comments: This question is designed to assess your ability to weigh up the results of the NEP with reference to its aims. Knowledge of the impact of the NEP will be expected. Sound answers will link results to aims and examine both economic and political aspects of the NEP. Better answers will develop these links in a sustained manner to provide an argument with a reasoned judgement on 'to what extent'.

A2 SECTION: THE RUSSIAN REVOLUTION AND THE ESTABLISHMENT OF BOLSHEVIK POWER

CONTEXT

Key questions
- Why did the Tsarist regime collapse in 1917?
- How and why were the Bolsheviks able to seize power in 1917?
- What direction did Bolshevik ideology and tactics take between 1903 and 1917?
- To what extent did practical difficulties stop Lenin from implementing communist ideology?
- What was the nature of the Bolshevik state?
- How important was the role of Lenin?
- How and why did Stalin manage to secure power by 1929?

The Russian Revolution of 1917 was one of the most important events of the twentieth century. It resulted in the collapse of the Tsarist regime and the establishment of the world's first communist state. Lenin has been seen as a symbol of the ability of the oppressed to throw off the shackles of capitalism and imperialism and take power for themselves. In this context, there has been a lot of debate amongst historians about the tumultous events of the Russian Revolution and its aftermath. The failure of Tsarism raised the question of whether there was any prospect of Tsarist Russia moving towards a form of democracy such as existed in the West. For those historians who see the fall of Tsarism as likely, even inevitable, the role of the Bolsheviks in bringing about its collapse and in taking the opportunities presented to them after 1917 has been a source of argument. Historians have examined the ideology and tactics of Lenin and the Bolshevik Party in an attempt to analyse why a small, minority group were able to seize power in one the world's largest states.

The consolidation of Bolshevik rule after 1917 has generated debate over the practicality of applying communist ideology to the real world. Was a workers' revolution sacrificed for the sake of the Bolshevik party's own power? Historians from alternative political and philosophical perspectives have reached different answers in response to this sort of question. Within the debate over the nature of the Bolshevik Revolution, and the regime that followed, has been a special focus on the role of Lenin and the influence he exerted on the course of events.

These historical issues are still influenced by present-day attitudes and to engage in this debate is to bring history alive.

SECTION 1

Why did the Tsarist regime collapse in 1917?

In order to analyse the collapse of Tsarism in Russia it is useful to focus on the range of issues which played a part in weakening the regime. The main factors responsible for its downfall can be divided into long-term, short-term and immediate causes.

LONG-TERM FACTORS

These include the following:

- **The system of autocracy**. The reliance on rule by one person, as that person sees fit, was beginning to look outdated by the early twentieth century. The growth of industry and with it new industrial classes (both middle class and working class) exaggerated the division between those with power and those without. A system based on government by the Tsar and his supporters from the landed aristocracy was under increasing pressure. The demand for a measure of parliamentary democracy was growing, especially from the middle classes and the liberal intelligentsia.
- **The personality of Nicholas II**. One of the weaknesses of a hereditary system, such as in Tsarist Russia, is that it is dependent on the line of inheritance rather than ability. As the last Tsar of Russia, Nicholas II was ill-suited to the role he had to play and the responsibilities of the role he had to take on. Weak, hesitant and reactionary, Nicholas found himself in a difficult and challenging position. His ability to rule effectively was also undermined by those around him who he relied upon for advice, his wife Alexandra and Rasputin. Would a person better suited to the demands of ruling Russia have fared any better?
- **The stresses and strains in Russian society**. Instead of focusing exclusively on the individual, it is also useful to consider the circumstances Nicholas II found himself in. The process of industrialisation had resulted in the growth of new classes – the middle-class factory owners and the industrial working class – and new social conditions. The rapid speed of industrialisation produced enormous tensions as appalling working and living conditions in the growing towns and cities bred discontent. Conditions in the countryside were little better and divisions between the kulaks and the poorer peasants remained a source of tension.
- **The growth of organised opposition**. The new economic and social conditions caused by rapid industrialisation were to aid the growth of

groups opposed to the Tsar. Although opposition to the regime was nothing new, the development of large industrial centres gave an added edge to revolutionary groups who targeted their ideas at the industrial worker. The Bolsheviks were just one of several groups who wished to see the eventual overthrow of the regime. Even so, these groups still have to be seen in their wider context. Support for them was limited and their members were more concerned with economic issues such as wages than radical political change. It must also be remembered that it was the peasantry, and not the industrial workers, that made up the vast bulk of the population and revolutionary groups found the peasants a harder group to organise.

SHORT-TERM FACTORS

- **The impact of the First World War.** Despite creating an initial wave of patriotism that strengthened the regime, the war was to create enormous pressure on the Tsar. The war caused social and economic dislocation as the regime grappled with food shortages, rising prices and the effects of supplying the vast military machine of the Russian Empire. As military defeats took their toll on resources and morale, the Tsar lost his key supporters. The war played a crucial role in the radicalisation of both the industrial workers and the peasants. It was these groups that had to endure harsh conditions brought on by the war at home or face the devastating realities of life at the front. Thus the concerns of the industrial workers and peasants coincided during the war with dangerous consequences for the government. As well as putting severe pressures on the regime, the war weakened its resilience. The government and its bureaucracy became so chaotic and poorly organised that the regime found it difficult to function with much degree of effectiveness. The actions of Alexandra and Rasputin during the war merely served to exacerbate this weakness. The personnel who made up the regime lost faith in Tsarism as an effective system for ruling the country. In this respect the war can be seen as a catalyst which helped speed up the collapse of an outdated system.

IMMEDIATE FACTORS

The factors which precipitated the final collapse of the system were:

- **Demonstrations and unrest** in the cities of Russia, especially in the capital Petrograd. These activities were driven largely by economic hardship. Most of the demonstrations were spontaneous, rather than organised by opposition groups.

- **The attitude and actions of the army.** Due to their loss of faith in the regime as a result of continued military failure in the war and sympathy for the hardships experienced by the demonstrators, the army refused to take action against the unrest. They also persuaded the Tsar to abdicate.
- **The decision of Nicholas II** to abdicate his position. As no replacement for the Tsar could be found within the Romanov family, the Tsarist regime finally came to an end.

In the final analysis, the Tsarist regime was not overthrown by revolutionary activity – the demonstrations of February 1917 were largely spontaneous and leaderless. The regime collapsed under the strains imposed on an already fragile system by the First World War. The long-term factors, which had weakened the regime, left it vulnerable to the additional strains imposed on it by the war. This short-term factor had resulted in hardships which affected both peasants and industrial workers, providing weight of numbers behind the growing unrest. This made the opposition much more dangerous than it had been in 1905. The immediate factor which caused the collapse of the regime was a combination of this unrest with a failure of the Tsar's own supporters to carry on propping up a regime in which they had lost faith. The war had stripped away the basis of support for the regime by alienating both the aristocrats in the government, who were demoralised by its descent into chaos, and the officers in the army, who had first-hand experience of military failure.

INTERPRETATIONS OF THE DOWNFALL OF TSARISM

The importance attached to each of these factors has been the source of much debate between historians. Where the emphasis has been placed has often depended on the philosophical background of the particular historian involved. Approaches can be divided into various schools of thought.

The liberal school

Until the 1970s the dominant school of historians in the West was that of the liberal tradition. These historians were influenced by the prevailing culture in the West, one of liberal democracy with its emphasis on political and religious freedom. When examining long-term factors in the Russian Revolution, liberal historians have traditionally been classed as 'optimists' who see the Tsarist regime in the years 1905-14 as making solid progress towards modernisation and reform. The result of this progress was to enhance the prospects of the regime's survival and they point to evidence which seems to show that the regime was resilient. This viewpoint has been well articulated by A. Gerschenkron in numerous books and articles. The evidence cited to support progress made by the regime centres on Russian economic performance after 1905 when considerable growth has been noted. Evidence of stability includes the effectiveness of the Tsar's machinery for repression and the limited nature of opposition. The 'optimists' point to apathy among the workers and the fact that many intellectuals became disheartened at the prospects for change due to the reforms introduced by the Tsar. To the revolutionaries within Russia these reforms and their economic success were seen as lessening the chances of revolution. Stolypin's land reforms could, it was felt, prevent the peasantry from becoming involved in revolutionary activity. The setting up of a national Duma, or parliament, after 1905 could have led the regime to evolve into a western-style liberal democracy with a constitutional monarchy. The prospects for the regime were seen as good. As Shidlovsky, a member of the Duma stated: 'Give us ten more years and we are safe'.

To the 'optimists' what shattered this progress and destabilised the regime was the First World War. They see the war as the main factor responsible for the collapse of the regime and the move to the political extreme, i.e. Bolshevism. It was, therefore, the war which led to unrest because of the food shortages and economic distress it brought. The role of the revolutionary groups is therefore played down. Indeed, the liberal school argues that the unrest of February 1917 was largely spontaneous and unorganised. To the 'optimist' school Bolshevism was not the answer to Russia's problems; they see the development of a liberal democracy on Western lines after 1905 as a possibility. Not surprisingly, this view was supported by Russian liberals such as P. Miliukov in *History of the Second Russian Revolution* (1921) and M. Florinsky in *The End of the Russian Empire* (1931). These writers saw the events of 1917 as a move away from the path of development that they had personally advocated. Later, these views were also presented from a more detached standpoint by L. Schapiro in *The Origin of the Communist Autocracy* (1955) and H. Seton-Watson's *The Russian Empire 1801–1917* (1967).

One important factor, which needs to be borne in mind when considering the liberal school of thought, is the type of sources used immediately after the Revolution. Many Russian liberals and members of the Russian upper class left Russia after the Revolution and settled in the West. In the 1920s these émigrés produced a wide range of memoirs and accounts of what they had witnessed. This group of people had a strong dislike for what had happened in 1917 and felt nostalgia for the past, for the Tsarist regime which had assured them of wealth and privilege. With Soviet archives inaccessible to those in the West, historians had to rely on this rather narrow range of sources.

One aspect on which the liberal school has been more critical is that of the role of Nicholas II. Liberal historians tend to stress the importance of individuals in the process of historical change and it has been, perhaps, of some comfort to blame the individual rather than the Tsarist system. The image presented of Nicholas II has been of a spineless autocrat isolated from the world that existed outside the palace.

The memoirs of people who were linked to the Imperial court do present a more favourable image of Nicholas, however. Pierre Gilliard, the French tutor to the Imperial family, presented a picture of a devoted family in his book *Thirteen Years at the Russian Court* (1921). Anna Vyrubova's *Memoirs of the Russian Court* (1923) confirmed this image although it is the view of a very naïve eye-witness. Her evidence was also attacked as a result of accusations that she was a mistress of Rasputin, rumours only scotched when she underwent a medical which proved she was a virgin. The memoirs of Baroness Isa Buxhoeveden, Alexandra's lady-in-waiting, were published in 1923 and attempted to present the royal couple as tragic, misunderstood figures. These writers were not, however, objective observers.

The 'pessimist' school

This 'optimist' viewpoint was challenged by some historians in the West who saw revolution in Russia as inevitable with or without the First World War. To the 'pessimists' the Tsarist regime was incapable of real change and the changes made were either too limited or even counter-productive. They point to the whittling away of concessions made after 1905, the failure of the Duma to develop into a meaningful parliament and the growth of opposition. Together this amounted to sham constitutionalism showing that the Tsar had no intention of relinquishing the autocratic powers which he possessed. The economic reforms of the Tsar are seen as causing stresses and strains in Russian society and leading to a more radical population in the towns and the countryside. To the 'pessimists' Nicholas II had learnt few lessons from the 1905 Revolution which had shown how vulnerable the regime was.

Historians in the West have, in general, been against the idea of 'inevitable revolution'. Yet there have been 'pessimists' in the West. E. H. Carr and W. E. Mosse, writing in the 1950s and 1960s, both stress the limitations of Stolypin's reforms and the consequent revolutionary potential of the workers and peasants. Historians in the West who see Tsarism as doomed before the war do not, however, see a Bolshevik Revolution as inevitable. They prefer to see a range of possibilities.

The Soviet school before 'glasnost'

In the traditional Marxist approach the role of the individual is not important and, therefore, the weaknesses of Nicholas II as Tsar of Russia

A Marxist view of Tsarist Russia. The layers of the 'cake' show, from the top: the Tsar and Tsarina; government ministers, 'We rule you'; the Church, 'We fool you'; the army, 'We shoot you'; the upper classes, 'We eat for you'. At the bottom, bearing the weight of the whole structure, are peasants and industrial workers, some of whom are beginning to protest.

are of little consequence to the process of historical change. Until the mid-1980s, the standard Soviet approach to the study of the Russian Revolution was based on the ideas of Marx and Lenin, who saw history as a process of a change brought about by class struggle. To Marx, historical change involved passing through various stages driven by socio-economic forces. To Marx, **feudalism** was the stage where power was in the hands of the landed class or aristocracy, who exercised control over the peasantry. He saw feudalism as giving way to **capitalism** where large-scale factory industry led to power being taken over by a new class of merchants and factory-owners (bourgeoisie) with a division between the bourgeoisie and the proletariat (industrial workers). The final revolution would be when the proletariat overthrows the bourgeoisie to abolish all private ownership and build a **socialist state** where every person's needs would be met. To Soviet historians this process was inevitable and determined by the 'laws of history'.

The Soviet school saw the last years of the Tsarist regime as a period when both the bourgeoisie and the proletariat were gaining economic power at the expense of the landed class, whose interests were represented by the Tsar's government. Thus, to Soviet writers, the fall of the Tsarist regime was merely part of an inevitable pattern of historical change brought about by class conflict. It would have happened with or without the First World War. The proletariat were not only becoming more class-conscious but were also becoming better organised. The role of the Bolshevik Party was seen as central in providing a vehicle for expressing the will of the industrial workers. This emphasis led to Soviet historians going to elaborate lengths to show Bolshevik activity in over 200 towns and amongst various groups in the armed forces. Not surprisingly, a lot of work has been done on the Vyborg district of Petrograd where the Bolsheviks were known to be relatively strong. In the traditional Soviet approach it was the growing pressure from the proletariat and peasants that led to the collapse of Tsarism. Yet because of the betrayal of the workers by moderate socialist groups such as the Mensheviks, who decided to work with the Provisional Government, the Bolshevik Revolution had to wait for another eight months.

The work of Revisionist historians

Since the mid-1980s and Gorbachev's policy of *glasnost*, Revisionist historians have been able to make use of the many new sources available. Their results have challenged the views of both the Liberal and Soviet schools. There have been two main approaches by Revisionists, each employing a different emphasis.

The first approach has been by **economic historians**, such as P. Gatrell in *The Tsarist Economy 1850-1917* (1986), who have shown that the Tsarist economy, in both industrial and agricultural production, performed very well indeed but that this had little impact on the peasant's traditional demand for land ownership or the industrial worker's demand for political representation. The potential for revolutionary activity is highlighted.

The second approach has been by **neo-populist social historians** who have emphasised the social structure within Russia and changes to it. They have highlighted factors in towns and the countryside that both promoted and reduced revolutionary potential. S. Smith, in *Red Petrograd*, (1983) has shown that the growth of revolutionary feeling among the workers in the capital city was evident before the First World

War. What the war did was to make this movement more political rather than focused on merely economic issues such as wages and jobs. Yet Smith has also shown that in February 1917 the industrial workers were far less organised than the Soviet view suggests. The amount of uncontrolled violence and robbery is used to support this as well as pointing to the weak position of the Bolsheviks. In fact, much of the revolutionary activity of early 1917 was due to the Mensheviks and SRs rather than the Bolsheviks. Divisions in the Bolshevik Party also put it in a weak position to take advantage of the events of February. The importance of the industrial workers in leading the unrest has been challenged by A. Wildman in *The End of the Russian Imperial Army* (1980). His work suggests that the soldiers' protests were the result of their own experiences rather than stirred up by workers' organisations. The same conclusion has been drawn for peasant protests.

Revisionists have also examined the role of the liberals and middle classes in February 1917. They have shown that the divisions within these groups weakened their chances of making a concerted effort to protect their position. The war did little to overcome differences in wealth and interests within the middle class which had existed before 1914.

When looking at the role of the Mensheviks and SRs the Revisionists have presented a more favourable and sympathetic picture than the Soviet view. The Bolshevik view that the other socialists threw in their lot with the middle-class parties is only true in some cases such as N. Sukhanov. Many Mensheviks were committed to using the situation presented in 1917 to promote workers' interests and developing their organisations.

Russian writers since 'glasnost'

Gorbachev's policy of *glasnost* (openness) not only led to a greater availability of sources for historians after 1985 but also to the Russians challenging their own views of the past. As the Soviet Union collapsed, Russians became highly critical of communism and looked back with renewed interest to the pre-revolutionary period, in an attempt to rediscover their history. This has led many Russian writers to present a far more sympathetic picture of Nicholas II. By 1998 there was even talk of Nicholas in terms of a Christian martyr deserving of sainthood. For most serious historians in the West this is seen as going too far. There is a difference to be made between the devout father and the inept ruler.

Revisionist historians have, however, provided some evidence which could be used in defence of Nicholas II. They have stressed the enormous difficulties confronting him and often make the point that these problems would have been a severe challenge for even a gifted Tsar. R. Manning in *Crisis of the Old Order* (1982) concludes that it was Tsarism which was at fault rather than the Tsar; the system had become deadlocked.

CONCLUSIONS

The greater availability of sources since 1985 has enabled previous viewpoints to be assessed with more confidence. The work of Revisionist historians has challenged many of the conclusions of earlier writers. They have been able to use the approaches of social and economic historians to highlight the 'revolution from below', i.e. the changes occurring amongst the Russian workers and peasants. The Revisionists have, nevertheless, been criticised by Liberal historians, for underestimating the impact of individuals, such as Nicholas II, and with it the importance of the revolution 'from above'. Although the view that the Tsarist regime was overthrown by revolutionary groups is hard to sustain when looking at the evidence, the situation appears to have been more complex than the early writings of the Liberal school had indicated. Tsarism collapsed due to a mixture of pressures both internal and external to the regime. The role of the First World War in bringing these tensions into sharp focus was to prove ultimately fatal to a government which was in need of stronger, more dynamic leadership.

SECTION 2

How and why were the Bolsheviks able to seize power in 1917?

It is often said that each generation rewrites its own history of the past, seeing in it that which reflects its own values and attitudes. Yet it is not just each generation which does this but each historian. The result of this is usually a diverse range of views and approaches adopted by historians to historical issues. On an event of such importance and so politically charged as the Bolshevik Revolution the debate has been very marked and sometimes fierce. Given the changes in Russia since the fall of communism and the opening of previously closed archives, this debate is still very lively and our views of 1917 are still subject to change. The following method of categorising key perspectives on the Bolshevik Revolution is based on those identified by Edward Acton in *Rethinking the Russian Revolution* (1990).

The Liberal school

When considering the October Revolution the Liberal school vigorously disputes the standard Soviet view, put forward before *glasnost* in the mid-1980s, that the Revolution was a popular rising. Instead, they see it as the result of a determined and ruthless group taking advantage of the unusual circumstances that occurred in October 1917. To the Liberal historian there was nothing inevitable about this revolution. It was the force of Lenin's personality and his political skill which enabled the Bolsheviks to make use of the chaos brought about by the impact of the First World War. Liberal historians see the Bolsheviks as a minority group who seized power by force because of their superior organisation and not because of mass support from the people. Growing support in the soviets for the Bolsheviks is dismissed, being seen as the result of manipulation and infiltration. Where support is evident it is viewed as due largely to the political backwardness of the peasants and workers. What gave the Bolsheviks the advantage was the chaotic situation of 1917 and Lenin's skilful opportunism. L. Schapiro in *The Origin of the Communist Autocracy* (1955) presents the October Revolution as a military operation with little popular involvement and as a result a dictatorship was imposed on the Russian people.

The Soviet school before 'glasnost'

The events of October 1917 were, according to the standard Soviet viewpoint, the next stage in the inevitable process of historical change driven by class conflict. Nonetheless, the Revolution was still seen as a

A still from Eisenstein's film 'October', showing the storming of the Winter Palace, October 1917.

Bolshevik triumph due to the party's role in organising the growing feeling of class consciousness in the proletariat and peasantry so that power could be seized in their name. From this viewpoint the role of Lenin is seen as important both in terms of his leadership and in his skilful strategy. The Bolsheviks were able to push for the demands of the proletariat and peasants (peace, land and bread) and win mass support. Thus, the October Revolution was seen as a popular rising which was guided by the Bolsheviks. This viewpoint was, of course, followed by the Soviet school for reasons of ideology. There are some who differ within this school of thought, for example Trotsky, who drew attention to the corrections of the course of revolution by Lenin.

The standard Soviet view was presented in *The History of the Communist Party of the Soviet Union* (1941), an official work directly sponsored and supervised by the Bolshevik Party. Other Soviet writers such as A. Avrekh (1968) and A. Shapkarin (1960) presented the Marxist line in more analytical academic works.

There was also the view of other socialist commentators who saw the Revolution as occurring too early, as a result of a rushed attempt to move towards socialism against the principles of Marx. This view has been put forward by Menshevik leaders V. Chernov in *The Great Russian Revolution* (1936) and T. Dan in *The Origins of Bolshevism* (1965), a viewpoint stemming from the ideological differences between the Mensheviks and Bolsheviks.

The Libertarian school

Ever since the October Revolution there have been writers in the West from the left of the political spectrum who were unhappy with the course of events in Russia following 1917. These writers have tended to see the Revolution as a heroic struggle of the workers to throw off all forms of authority until the Bolsheviks betrayed them. October 1917 signalled, according to this school of thought, the imposition of Bolshevik control over the masses and an end of the challenge to authority. The liberty of the masses had been stamped on, this time by the Bolsheviks rather than by Tsarism. These writers have often been anarchists who detest all kinds of authority. The rise of the New Left in the 1960s, in response to criticisms of liberal democracy generated in the West by the Vietnam War, tended to encourage this line of thought. Given the problem of the lack of access to Soviet sources before *glasnost*, most of these works were subjective and lacking in evidence. Although heavily criticised as 'trendy lefties' some, but not all, of their conclusions that the Bolsheviks imposed their will on workers' organisations have been partly supported by Revisionist historians since 1985.

The work of Revisionist historians

The approach adopted by many Revisionists has been that of neo-populist social historians. Their emphasis has been on structural changes in society. They have shown that in the countryside and in the industrial areas there were factors at work that created greater social differences and produced unrest but there were also factors that worked to reduce these divisions. For example, trade unions could have worked either to push for revolutionary change or to restrain and moderate workers to help capitalism develop more smoothly. Historians such as H. Hogan (1983) and D. Mandel (1983) have looked at the attitudes of industrial workers in Petrograd and the level of Bolshevik influence over them. Their studies show differences in the level of militancy depending on a range of social issues such as level of education, whether skilled or unskilled and which type of industry they worked in.

Research by the Revisionists on the October Revolution specifically has tended to examine the role of the industrial workers and peasants to assess the amount of popular support for the Bolsheviks. Was October 1917 a 'revolution from below'? S. A. Smith (1983) has shown that it is misleading to talk of the workers as a unified group all with the same experiences. He has also revealed the range of workers' demands, many of them economic. Yet it is clear that there was an increase in revolutionary feeling among these different groups. In addition, Revisionists have looked at the organisation of the Bolshevik Party to see how this related to the increase in revolutionary attitudes. A. Rabinowitch in *The Bolsheviks come to power* (1976) has shown that the Bolsheviks were not as unified and disciplined as often presented. The growth in membership during 1917 made these divisions greater as many new members were ex-Mensheviks and ex-SRs, each with different ideas. Even among the leadership there were divisions over strategy, as the arguments between Lenin and Kamenev and Zinoviev over the decision to stage the Revolution show. Organisational problems were made more difficult because the Bolsheviks' communication networks were irregular and unreliable. Nonetheless, the Bolsheviks had a growing base of support in the soviets. What they were good at doing was making their aims coincide with those of the workers and peasants. Rather than create the revolutionary attitudes of the workers they merely articulated them. This was, perhaps, another example of Lenin's skilful opportunism.

The thrust of much of the Revisionist work has qualified both the liberal interpretation of the October Revolution as a *coup* by a small well-organised minority and the standard Soviet view that it was a popular rising. The Revisionists show that the Bolsheviks owed their success not to their superior discipline and organisation or mass support but to an ability to use their base in the soviets to promote popular demands and to react rapidly to events, making the most of opportunities as they presented themselves.

Russian writers since 'glasnost'

When Gorbachev became leader of the Soviet Union in 1985 he launched a policy of *glasnost*, or openness, which encouraged a more critical approach to the past and this, coupled with the collapse of the communist system in 1991, has led to a wider range of views from Russian writers. The trend most evident amongst Russian commentators has been towards a more critical view of the Bolsheviks and everything they stood for. The Revolution is now seen by many Russians as an event which led to their enslavement by an armed minority.

Conclusions

It is clear that the more recent Revisionist approaches have benefited from the opening up of Russian archives since *glasnost* and the later collapse of the Soviet Union. This has made it much easier to study developments at a more localised level and to gain enough statistical information to make the application of the quantitative methods of social history more meaningful. These approaches can focus on revolution 'from below', i.e. the changes and developments occurring amongst Russian workers and peasants. The evidence from this approach points to a more active role by the workers and peasants in the Revolution than earlier Liberal writers had acknowledged. The result has been to challenge many of the assumptions of earlier interpretations that the October Revolution did not amount to much more than the seizure of power by an armed minority who imposed their will on the Russian masses. The Revisionists have also drawn attention to the role of the Bolsheviks in guiding and directing the revolutionary forces to achieve this seizure of power, which might not otherwise have happened. In this sense the October Revolution was the result of actions by an armed minority whose views were skilfully aligned, however briefly, with those of the workers and peasants.

Summary of interpretations of the Bolshevik Revolution

Key issue: Was the October Revolution a seizure of power by a small, well-organised group or a popular rising?

The Soviet school before glasnost (mid-1980s)

VIEW:
- Sees the Bolshevik Revolution as the next stage in an inevitable process of historical change driven by class conflict.
- Sees the October Revolution as a popular rising.

WHY:
- Used to justify the position of the Bolshevik Party in power, thus it became the official line before *glasnost*.
- Selected evidence to support Bolshevik support, e.g. factories in the Vyborg district.

VALUE:
- Stresses the level of support the Bolsheviks had but this tends to be exaggerated due to the selection of evidence from pro-Bolshevik areas.

The Liberal school

VIEW:
- Vigorously disputes the view of October 1917 as a popular rising.
- Sees the Revolution as a seizure of power by a small, well-organised group.
- Highlights the role of Lenin as a skilful manipulator of the situation in 1917.

WHY:
- Put forward by historians in the West who saw Bolshevik rule as an attack on the values of liberal democracy (e.g. political and religious freedom) which dominate political systems in the West.
- Heavy reliance on the evidence of émigrés who were critical of the Bolsheviks.

VALUE:
- Draws attention to the role of key individuals, i.e. Lenin and Trotsky.
- But tends to dismiss/underestimate evidence of support for the Bolsheviks.

The Libertarian school

VIEW:

• The revolutionary movement was hijacked by the Bolsheviks for their own ends. Bolshevik rule was imposed on the masses.

WHY:

• This view put forward by those on the left who were disillusioned by the Bolsheviks, e.g. Anarchists, or later (1960s) by those of the New Left who disliked authoritarianism and saw it in the Bolsheviks.

VALUE:

• Challenges the underlying assumptions of the Liberal school
• But based either on evidence from people who had suffered at the hands of the Bolsheviks or little evidence at all.

The Revisionist school

VIEW:

• There was some support for the Bolsheviks from the masses, but the pattern of support is more complex than either the Liberal or Soviet schools acknowledge.
• The Bolsheviks were able to articulate the demands of the masses to their own advantage.

WHY:

• They look at the role of the workers and peasants in the Revolution – the 'Revolution from below'.
• New sources available since *glasnost* which make social history more meaningful.

VALUE:

• Highlights the role of the workers and peasants in the Revolution.
• Based on a much wider range of sources than books written before *glasnost*.

Russian views since glasnost

VIEW:

• More critical of standard Soviet view of mass support for the Bolsheviks.
• More critical of the achievements of the Bolsheviks

WHY:

• *Glasnost* encouraged a wider range of views; writers did not have to accept the standard view.
• Since the rejection of communism in Russia in 1991 there has been a rejection of claims by the Bolsheviks, including that of mass support.

- Greater availability of sources previously suppressed by the Soviet Government.

VALUE:
- Presents the view of those most affected by the legacy of the Revolution.
- But very critical of the Bolshevik Party.
- Tends to downplay evidence of mass support of Bolsheviks.

SECTION 3

What direction did Bolshevik ideology and tactics take between 1903 and 1917?

The development of Bolshevik ideology and the tactics used to promote it were based on the ideas of Karl Marx. Marx had developed his ideas whilst observing the progress of capitalism during the enormous industrial growth of the early nineteenth century in Western Europe. His theories were based upon the trends evident in the most advanced industrial nations of his time. It is, therefore, not surprising that when applied to less-developed economies, such as Russia in the early twentieth century, modifications and adaptations of his principles were needed. Lenin was to take the ideas of Marx and adapt them to the reality of the situation facing the Bolsheviks in Russia.

WHAT WERE THE MAIN PRINCIPLES OF MARXIST THEORY?

Although born to a Jewish family in Germany in 1818, Karl Marx spent most of his life in exile in Britain. His ideas were put forward in two key books: *The Communist Manifesto* (1848) and *Das Kapital* (1867-90). Much of his later work was written in collaboration with his friend Friedrich Engels. In attempting to describe capitalism and the exploitation it produced, both Marx and Engels based their work on conditions in Britain during the mid-nineteenth century. This was a natural consequence of their own experiences, yet it did not mean that their observations were equally applicable to other countries at different stages of development.

The main principles of Marxism were:

The idea of class struggle

Marx explained social and political relationships in terms of material needs. Humans require food, goods and services in order to survive. According to Marx, history was a series of struggles by one class against another to obtain these material needs and it was this that produced change in history. Those without power were seen by Marx as alienated from society and politics; as they were forced into an economic position (performing labour for others) which took away their freedom. It was in the interests of those with power to maintain their position and privileges in society; therefore they would not give up power without a struggle.

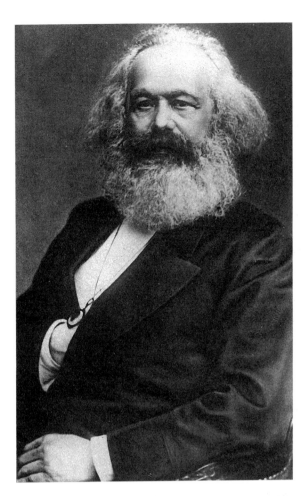

Karl Marx.

Thus, classes were always hostile to each other and this affected the nature of change when it occurred.

The inevitability of historical change

Marx saw historical change as passing through various stages driven by socio-economic forces. These stages were as follows:

1 **Primitive communism.** Humans lived in primitive communities where there were no social classes and no concept of private property. This stage can be seen in many Stone Age groups, where humans lived in collective groups. This phase would give way to one based on ownership of land and the development of social classes.

2 **Feudalism.** In this phase, society would be controlled by the land-owning aristocracy. Their power would be based on their ownership of land and would be exercised over the peasantry, those who worked the land. Land produced food, a basic requirement to support a pre-industrial population. A surplus of food would enable a section of

society to engage in other activities. As trade and industry grew feudalism would be replaced by capitalism.

3 **Capitalism.** The growth of trade and industry produced two new classes: the bourgeoisie (factory owners and merchants) and the proletariat (industrial workers). The bourgeoisie became powerful because they owned the means of production (i.e. factories), the means of distribution (e.g. railways, shops) and the means of exchange (banks). The proletariat had to rely on selling themselves as labour to the bourgeoisie to gain enough money to survive. Marx saw this relationship as one of exploitation; the proletariat being deprived of a fair wage by the bourgeoisie who pocketed the profit made from goods and services. The proletariat were forced to live and work in appalling conditions as powerless cogs in a vast industrial process. Thus, the bourgeoisie grew rich at the expense of the proletariat, who were cheated of their just rewards.

As capitalism progressed, this exploitation would become more and more obvious and unacceptable to the proletariat, who would rise up by their own efforts and get rid of the bourgeoisie in order to get a fair share of the goods and services they helped produce. This would lead to a new phase in historical development.

4 **Socialism.** In this phase workers' organisations would form a Dictatorship of the Proletariat to rule on their own behalf. Food, goods and services would be distributed fairly according to need. In this respect, socialism would enable humans to enjoy the level of material production achieved by capitalism. As material needs were met there would be no need for competition. As competition faded mankind would reach its ultimate destiny.

5 **Communism.** With no shortage of goods there would be less need to regulate society. Government would be unnecessary and would gradually 'wither away'. Co-operation would replace competition in a classless society based on the economic principle of 'From each according to his ability, to each according to his needs'. The result would be a class-less and state-less society.

The key principle behind this process of historical change was, according to Marx, its inevitability. Change was governed by a series of historical laws, much like scientific laws, which could not be altered. This idea that history is shaped by socio-economic forces outside our control is often referred to as **determinism**. Thus, to Marx, the collapse of capitalism was inevitable. Marx's vision of the transitional socialist phase and the communist ideal were vague. This was to provide the followers of Marx with the opportunity to interpret his ideas in different ways.

HOW DID LENIN ADAPT MARXIST THEORY TO THE SITUATION IN RUSSIA?

Marx had seen the proletarian revolution occurring in those countries where capitalism was at its most advanced. Those countries that seemed ripe for revolution were therefore to be found in Western Europe, such as Britain and Germany. In the early twentieth century Russia was still semi-feudal with little industrial development. For those who wished to see revolution in Russia, according to Marx's theory, the signs were not good, for the following reasons:

- **The lack of capitalist development.** The bourgeoisie seemed incapable of carrying out their own revolution. Power remained in the hands of the Tsar and his supporters from the landed aristocracy. How could a socialist revolution be expected before capitalism had developed?
- **The limited size of the proletariat.** Small-scale industrial development had failed to produce an industrial workforce of a size sufficient to have the potential for revolution.
- **The lack of an organised proletariat.** The industrial workforce that did exist lacked those elements Marx saw as necessary to galvanise themselves into action, e.g. education at a level that would raise awareness of their own position. The repressive measures of the Tsarist regime made the formation of workers' organisations extremely difficult.

Lenin was to make adaptations to Marxist theory in the light of these factors. In practice, the application of Marxism to the Russian experience was to divide revolutionary groups. These divisions were often widened by the way in which ideas from other radical groups were incorporated into debates. There were arguments over whether capitalist development should be aided in order to speed up the process of historical change or whether the circumstances could be used to promote proletarian revolution without further delay. Lenin's interpretation of Marxist theory was as follows:

1 **Do not delay the Revolution.** Lenin believed that the Revolution need not be delayed until capitalism had developed. This was a direct attack on the view of other revolutionary groups, such as the Mensheviks, who believed that the way forward was to work with the bourgeoisie to improve workers' conditions, whilst waiting for capitalism to collapse. There was, Lenin argued, little point in using the democratic process to promote the interests of the industrial workers when, under the Tsarist regime, there were no real democratic institutions to use.

2 **The role of the peasantry.** To Marx, the idea of revolution was based firmly around the proletariat, rejecting those who saw revolutionary

potential in the peasantry, and Lenin's early writings echoed this view. Yet in Russia the lack of an organised proletariat posed a particular problem. The vast majority of the population were peasants and Russian radicals had long since debated their role in revolution. The *narodniks* of the nineteenth century had believed in the theory of peasant revolution and, although Marxists rejected this notion, some revolutionaries, such as the SRs, believed the peasantry could be harnessed to the cause of proletarian revolution. The harsh conditions under which the peasantry worked and lived gave them some common ground with the industrial workers. Both the peasants and the industrial workers could be seen as oppressed classes. It was not until 1917 that Lenin's writings show a change in his view towards the peasantry. Sometimes he used the term 'proletariat' to include poorer peasants and during the summer of 1917 Bolshevik propaganda was often targeted at the peasantry when their interests coincided with those of the industrial workforce.

3 **The Party as the vanguard of the Revolution.** If the proletariat was unable to carry out its own revolution, it could be achieved by the organisation of a highly centralised and disciplined party on their behalf. To Lenin, this was best achieved by a group of intellectuals dedicated to furthering the interests of the industrial workers. This group would be small enough to maintain the secrecy necessary against the Tsar's secret police. It would be the role of this party to speed up the process of historical change by direct intervention, i.e. by organising revolution. The Revolutionary Party would act as the vanguard of the Revolution, steering it to a successful conclusion. This view, first outlined in *What is to be done?* in 1902, differed from Marx's opinion that the Revolution would be based on the proletariat's own efforts. Very few Marxists believed that a small elite of revolutionaries would ever be able to carry out a successful revolution. To Lenin, it was the only way of overcoming the limitations of the Russian proletariat. This difference over tactics was to lead to the split between the Bolsheviks and Mensheviks in 1903.

4 **Russia as the weakest link in the capitalist system.** Whereas Marx had seen the potential for revolution as greater in the more advanced capitalist countries, Lenin saw the possibilities for attacking capitalism's weakest link. In *Imperialism: the Highest Stage of Capitalism* (1916) Lenin had developed Marx's idea on the capitalist system's use of foreign expansion to further its own existence. Marx had stated that capitalism would seize foreign territories in order to exploit their economic resources. Lenin believed that these resources had been used to buy off the workers by enabling the capitalist countries to improve working conditions and, therefore, reduce the revolutionary tendencies of the workforce. In this respect Russia was a weak link in the capitalist

system because it had failed to exploit foreign territories as effectively as Britain, France and Germany.

5 **The Dictatorship of the Proletariat.** Lenin saw this phase as a seizure of power by the party on behalf of the industrial workers. The party would form a dictatorship in order to ensure the Revolution survived in the face of counter-attacks by the bourgeoisie. Given the power of the bourgeoisie, this would require violence to be used and the party should not flinch from this. The use of violent action divided Lenin from other Marxists, such as Plekhanov, but it had been a notable feature of the Russian Populist movement of the nineteenth century. The Dictatorship of the Proletariat would also promote socialism by removing private ownership and by the state taking over the economy to be run in the interests of the workers. When the risk of counter-revolution was dealt with Lenin believed that the state would wither away and communism would develop. The result would be as Marx had indicated but the role to be played by the Dictatorship of the Proletariat was very much Lenin's own view.

Lenin's main works include *What is to be done?* (1902), *Imperialism: the Highest Stage of Capitalism* (1916) and *The State and Revolution* (1917). He was a prolific writer, whose collected works amounted to fifty-five volumes. The fact that in the Soviet Union the ideology of the state was referred to as Marxism-Leninism gives an indication of the importance attached to Lenin's ideas. Nonetheless, it would be wrong to view Lenin as primarily a theorist, he was above all else a practical politician. His ideas and interpretation of Marxism need to be seen within this context. In *The Bolshevik Revolution* (1950) E. H. Carr drew attention to Lenin's 'greatness as a political strategist and as a political tactician' who used his writings to carefully build up his position in advance, and his instinct to know 'where and when and how to strike or to hold back'.

One important example of Lenin's application of Marxist theory to the reality the Bolsheviks faced is the 'April Theses' of 1917. This article, published in *Pravda*, the party newspaper, was short and to the point. It was, as might be expected, more propaganda aimed at the Provisional Government than Marxist theory. Although it was written from the Marxist perspective of historical change, Lenin called for immediate proletarian revolution. This was seen by other revolutionaries, including some Bolsheviks, as moving away from a rigid Marxist approach. The 'April Theses' also contained a carefully prepared appeal to the industrial workers, peasants and soldiers: 'Peace, Bread and Land'. These were the three basic needs that urgently needed addressing during the chaotic months of the summer of 1917 and demonstrated Lenin's skill in translating Bolshevik ideas into accessible slogans which were so in tune with the demands of the Russian masses.

Lenin was able to adapt the basic principles of Marxist theory to the situation facing the Bolsheviks in Russia during the early part of the twentieth century. These modifications reflected an awareness of the peculiarities of the Russian context: both the reality of circumstances as well as the traditions of Russian radicalism. As a result his adaptations showed some significant divergences from Marxist theory in terms of the way forward for the Revolution. Lenin was not prepared to wait for the inevitable process of history to occur. He was ready to use the Bolshevik Party as an instrument of intervention to speed up the historical process in Russia.

SECTION 4

To what extent did practical difficulties stop Lenin from implementing communist ideology?

Communist ideology was seen by the Bolsheviks as the basis for creating a new social order, a utopia which represented human endeavour at its highest. Theoretical ideas were relatively easy to formulate and talk about; it was much harder to apply them to the real world as it existed in Russia after October 1917. Although Lenin can be regarded as a theorist, he was more importantly a political realist. He was prepared to make concessions and compromises where they were seen as essential to ensure the survival of the Bolshevik Revolution. By 1924, significant changes had been made to Bolshevik policy, many of which seemed less obviously tied to ideological considerations.

The writings of Lenin presented detailed assessments of the evils of capitalism and the need for revolution; ideas on what to do when in power were more vague. Lenin had outlined some of the key steps which should be taken to promote the development of socialism by a Dictatorship of the Proletariat. He called for the abolition of private ownership and the nationalisation of the means of production, distribution and exchange. The economy would, therefore, be placed in the hands of the government 'on behalf of the people'. This would allow goods to be distributed fairly according to need. Social classes would start to disappear as greater equality was achieved. The government would use its power and that of the state to deal with the threat of counter-revolution, after which the state would wither away. The result would be the creation of communism in practice. How and when these developments would take place was unclear and this was to provide some flexibility when the Bolsheviks tried to justify their policies by reference to ideology.

The Treaty of Brest-Litovsk (1918)

The Treaty which saw Russia pull out of the First World War was the first significant clash the Bolsheviks faced between ideological considerations and practical difficulties. Many in the Bolshevik leadership were ready to believe that Marx's idea of international proletarian revolution was about to be achieved. The chaos caused by the First World War had resulted in a series of demonstrations and unrest by workers across Europe, the most notable being in Germany. If the imperialist, capitalist nations of Western Europe were to be swept away then there seemed little point in signing a peace agreement with a German government that represented a capitalist state. Did the Bolshevik government have a duty to carry on fighting against capitalist imperialism? Many in the Bolshevik Party felt they did. Lenin, however, disagreed with this analysis. He argued that unless Russia was pulled out of the war, the Revolution would not survive. He recognised that the Bolsheviks' hold on power was still rather tenuous. In early 1918 the control exercised by the party only extended to the main cities of Russia. Lenin was aware that those Russians who were against the Revolution were likely to rally their supporters in an attempt to defeat the Bolsheviks. Peace with Germany was essential if the Bolsheviks were to consolidate their position and hold onto power.

Despite strong opposition from Bukharin and the Bolshevik Central Committee, Lenin was able to impose his view. The Treaty of Brest-Litovsk was signed in March 1918. Lenin's victory was particularly significant because in accepting the treaty the Bolsheviks had to give away over 32 per cent of Russia's agricultural land and 54 per cent of its industry. It was a bitter pill to swallow. Lenin did try to justify the treaty in ideological terms. When the international proletarian revolution took place in the future, Russia would regain the lost territories but the immediate priority was to ensure the Revolution survived in Russia. An underlying yet highly significant consideration was the recognition that the Russian armed forces were in no fit state to continue fighting in the war. This practical difficulty brought the issue into sharp focus.

Economic policy

The economic situation inherited by the Bolsheviks was extremely difficult. The economy had been ruined by the impact of the First World War and the Civil War that followed was to add to the economic chaos and dislocation. These circumstances were to present enormous practical difficulties to the Bolsheviks.

Initial economic policies. On coming to power the Bolsheviks issued a rush of decrees which seemed to be driven by ideological considerations. The Land Decree of 1917 abolished all private ownership of land; workers' control was established over industry. These were moves, undertaken when hopes and excitement were high, that pleased the more radical wing of the Bolshevik Party. The underlying reasons for these measures are less clear cut. The distribution of land to the peasants was not as radical a move as it seemed. It merely recognised by decree what had already taken place amidst the chaos at the end of the First World War. The establishment of workers' committees to control industry was more radical but the government also seems to have been aware of its own naïvety in this respect. It moved quickly to impose a measure of government control over industry through the setting up of the Supreme Council of the National Economy.

War Communism. Those measures introduced in 1918 to restore order and discipline to the economy in the face of Civil War became known as War Communism. They included the nationalisation of all sectors of industry, state control over trade and the requisitioning of food from the peasantry. War Communism shows the Bolsheviks responding to both practical difficulties and ideological considerations. Many Bolsheviks greeted the abolition of private enterprise as an important step towards socialism but it was also a sign of the government trying to establish firm direction over the economy in order to ensure sufficient supplies during the Civil War. In addition, it was a recognition that some of the early reforms had been too idealistic and that giving control to the workers had proved unworkable, especially during the emergency situation of the Civil War. The advantage for the Bolsheviks of War Communism was that practical necessities could often be justified by ideological considerations. It was not always to be so easy.

The New Economic Policy (1921). The NEP saw the reintroduction of capitalist elements into the economy. Small-scale industry and trade were returned to private ownership and the forced requisitioning of grain was brought to an end. To those on the left of the party, this marked a betrayal of the Revolution and Bolshevik ideology. To Lenin it marked a temporary but necessary step backwards in order to ensure the Revolution survived in the long term. The Bolsheviks had faced a combination of factors in 1921 that made their survival in government seem unlikely. The unpopularity of the harsh measures introduced under War Communism had resulted in the Tambov Rising and the Kronstadt Mutiny. The Tambov Rising was a response from the peasants to the forced requisitioning of their grain to feed the towns and the Red Army. The Kronstadt Mutiny was over the increased power of the party and was particularly significant as it involved sailors at the naval base who had been previously loyal to the Bolsheviks. These two events were to pose a serious practical difficulty for the Bolsheviks. In Lenin's own words, they 'lit up reality like a flash of lightning'. It was in response to this situation, coupled with the continued failure of the economy to recover, that Lenin introduced the NEP. Under the NEP unrest was reduced and the economy gradually started to improve. The charge of the Left, that the NEP had betrayed the Revolution, could be supported by the fact that it led to the reintroduction of a bourgeoisie: the Nepmen, kulaks and so-called '**bourgeois experts**'. It would, however, be misleading to see the NEP merely in this light. Heavy industry and the banks were kept firmly in government hands and the NEP was accompanied by a substantial increase in the political power and control of the government.

KEY TERM

Bourgeois experts A term used by Bolsheviks to describe former managers and owners of industry who were given jobs after nationalisation because they possessed skills and expertise which were desperately needed. The 'bourgeois experts' were resented by many industrial workers because, although few of them were Bolsheviks, they retained positions of importance.

A flourishing private market under the NEP.

Nonetheless, Lenin had shown his skills as a pragmatist, willing to compromise ideology in the short term to ensure long-term gain.

The retreat to capitalism under the NEP can also be seen as a reflection on the validity of Bolshevik ideology. Had Lenin been wrong to assume that socialism could be achieved without going through a stage of capitalist development first? The NEP can be seen as an acknowledgement that the Russian economy had not been ready for socialism. Were the Mensheviks correct in this respect after all?

The role of women

The balance between ideology and pragmatism is also shown in aspects of social policy. Bolshevik policies aimed at women and the family can give the impression that they were driven by ideological considerations. The relaxation of divorce law, the legalisation of abortion and the opening of crèches: these were all moves which gave women greater freedom. They were also introduced in order to encourage women into work during the Civil War. The importance of practical considerations over ideology is shown by the reversal of many of these measures after the Civil War was won. Bolshevik commitment to improving the position of women might also be questioned in the light of their weak challenge to the male-dominated society of the Muslim areas of Central Asia. Here traditional values posed considerable practical problems for the Bolsheviks. More tellingly, the Bolshevik record on promoting women within their own ranks in the Party was even less impressive.

Religion and the Orthodox Church

When dealing with the Russian Orthodox Church, practical considerations and ideology pushed the Bolsheviks in the same direction. To the communists religion was seen as little more than an alternative ideology, which was used as a method of social control to keep order amongst the population and uphold the old regime. As the Orthodox Church had been one of the 'pillars of Tsarism', owing its loyalty to the Tsar, it was necessary for the Bolsheviks to reduce its power and influence radically. This explains the harsh measures taken against the Church during the Civil War when the threat of counter-revolution was at its strongest. After the war the Bolsheviks felt able to adopt a softer approach which allowed worship to continue. This was, perhaps, a recognition by the Bolsheviks of the continuing influence of Christianity.

When dealing with Islam in the Central Asian region of the country the Bolsheviks were more conciliatory. Islam had not been closely associated with the Tsarist regime but it maintained a strong hold over the peoples of Central Asia. The Bolsheviks seemed to lack the confidence needed to reduce the powerful influence of Islamic traditions. Some desperate attempts were made by the party to use excerpts from the Koran, which emphasised communal living, to spread communist ideas but in general religious interference was minimal. The Bolsheviks had decided, reluctantly, to tolerate, rather than abolish, religion.

The Dictatorship of the Proletariat

The threat of counter-revolution had posed a serious threat to the survival of the Revolution and in response to this Lenin was to use the machinery of the party and the state in order to protect the interests of the proletariat. In this sense the Bolshevik regime implemented the political strategies outlined in Lenin's writings. The results of these strategies were to display trends that were uncomfortable for some Bolsheviks.

The use of violence. The expansion of the Cheka as an instrument of terror was the most obvious sign of this use of violence. The official figure for executions in 1918 was 6,300 and this was probably an underestimation. Lenin justified the use of terror by the need to ensure the Revolution did not fall to hostile forces. In the years of the Civil War this claim rang true but it was a tactic which some Bolsheviks shied away from. Marx had not advocated terror and Russian Marxists, such as Plekhanov, would have been appalled at its use.

The growth of the bureaucracy. Lenin's claim that the state would 'wither away' under socialism did not materialise. In reality the state saw enormous growth and both the party and state bureaucracy grew in power and in numbers. This development was criticised by Trotsky and Lenin. Both men were concerned about the bureaucracy administering for its own ends rather than those of the Revolution. Despite these concerns Lenin was aware that the Bolshevik Revolution could not be achieved without administrative machinery since the proletariat were seen as incapable of self-organisation for this purpose. It is, however, misleading to think that the Bolshevik rank and file saw the party apparatus as a self-serving bureaucracy in the Marxist sense. Sheila Fitzpatrick (1994) has drawn attention to the fact that the party bureaucracy was not specialised, generally it did not defer to professional experts and it did not go 'by the book'. This was a bureaucracy that was more likely to serve the interests of the Revolution.

It is clear by looking at the policies of the Bolsheviks that they faced enormous practical difficulties in implementing communist ideology. They were not only confused about how to achieve their 'brave new world' but also willing to retreat from communist ideology if it was in their short-term interest. Lenin was not merely a theorist but also a political strategist. As Lenin himself remarked: 'It is more pleasant and more useful to live through the experience of a revolution than to write about it'. Of course, all policies were dressed up in ideological terms but this was easier for some than for others, such as the NEP. As a last resort, the need to ensure the survival of the party in power – and with it the Revolution – could be used as a justification which merged ideology with pragmatism.

SECTION 5

What was the nature of the Bolshevik state?

According to Lenin, the Bolshevik regime, established after the October Revolution, was to act as a Dictatorship of the Proletariat. As such it would work in the interests of 'the people' to ensure that socialism was achieved in the face of the threat from counter-revolutionaries. During the Civil War that emerged after the Bolshevik seizure of power there was a need for strong leadership and harsh measures. This situation pushed the Bolsheviks into a militaristic approach which led to the establishment of a dictatorship by the party. Historians have argued about the nature of Bolshevik rule. Was it little more than a dictatorship of the Bolshevik Party, rather than of the proletariat? Was it Lenin's intention to set up such a dictatorship that, due to the dominant role he played, saw him emerge as a dictator?

The term 'dictatorship' is commonly used to denote a form of government that restricts traditional freedoms and ensures that authority from one source is maintained to the exclusion of all others. When considering the nature of Bolshevik rule it is important to differentiate between the idea of the Dictatorship of the Proletariat, as articulated by Lenin, and other forms of dictatorship. It would be unfair to condemn Lenin for setting up a system of government he had himself declared to be a necessary stage in the development of socialism. It is more fruitful to compare the nature of the government established by the Bolsheviks with the aims and intentions which lay behind it.

WHAT EVIDENCE CAN BE USED TO SUPPORT THE CLAIM THAT LENIN WAS A DICTATOR?

The removal of freedoms granted by the Provisional Government

The view that Lenin was a dictator is often based on the notion that the Bolsheviks took away the political and religious freedoms and rights briefly given during the Provisional Government, which was set up after the fall of the Tsarist regime. The Bolsheviks, however, argued that the Provisional Government was merely an instrument of the bourgeoisie, whose purpose was to maintain a capitalist system that exploited and oppressed the industrial workers. In addition, the Provisional Government had not been elected and therefore had no legitimate right to power. In this respect the Bolsheviks argued that their Dictatorship of the Proletariat would be a greater guarantee of the freedoms and rights of the workers.

The imposition of Bolshevik control over the Soviets

To many on the Left in Russia the February Revolution had paved the way for workers to gain control over the factories through the setting up of soviets, workers' councils to replace management and owners. The Bolsheviks initially consolidated this trend by giving control of the factories to workers' councils, but they reversed this system when they implemented War Communism. The return to hierarchical management structures, often using the former managers and owners of factories, was seen by those on the Left as the end of self-organisation by the workers. The slogan of 'Soviets without Bolsheviks', used during the Kronstadt Mutiny of 1921, indicated the resentment caused by the increase in power of the Bolshevik Party at the expense of the workers. This 'symbolic parting of the ways between the working class and the Bolshevik Party', as Sheila Fitzpatrick has described it, was to highlight the increasing authoritarian nature of the regime.

To Lenin the reimposition of management and the increase in party control was justified by the desperate need to ensure adequate production during the Civil War. Workers' councils were seen to have failed to produce effective industrial discipline and there were concerns about their lack of technical and management expertise. The pressures of the Civil War made this an important issue.

The creation of a one-party state

There is little doubt that Lenin always intended to create a one-party state although this was not true of some of his colleagues. If socialism was to be established then the Bolshevik Party needed to guard against counter-revolutionaries in all their forms. Lenin's idea of the party as the vanguard of the Revolution, steering it to a successful outcome, seemed to make a one-party state an inevitable conclusion. In establishing the one-party state the Bolsheviks did not implement a firm plan of action; it was through a series of ad hoc measures.

The destruction of the Constituent Assembly. The Constituent Assembly was to be a brief excursion into the politics of liberal democracy. The Assembly was elected according to the principle of universal suffrage (one person, one vote) and the Bolsheviks, although anxious about the likely outcome, were committed to holding the elections in November 1917. The results were as follows:

Lenin and the Russian Revolution

The results of the elections for the Constituent Assembly, November 1918

	Votes	Number of seats	Percentage of the vote
SRs	21.8 million	410	53%
Bolsheviks	10.0 million	175	24%
Kadets	2.1 million	17	5%
Mensheviks	1.4 million	18	3%
Others/unaccounted	6.3 million	62	15%

Despite divisions amongst the SRs, they had won a comfortable majority in the elections. On these results the Bolsheviks had been rejected by the voters. However, Lenin dissolved the Constituent Assembly within days of its first meeting and used in its place the All-Russian Congress of Soviets, a body where Bolshevik support was greater. Such actions seemed to show a tendency towards political dictatorship by the Bolsheviks although Lenin justified them by drawing attention to Bolshevik success in the large industrial cities, where they had beaten the other parties: 'Where the town inevitably leads the country; the country inevitably follows the town'. This implied that the Bolsheviks had won the election – if only you looked hard enough at the results.

The destruction of other political parties. In early 1918 the Bolsheviks aimed to restrict the other political parties by making it difficult for them to get their message across: the dissolution of the Constituent Assembly deprived the other parties of a valuable platform. The removal of the vote from 'bourgeois classes', such as employers and priests, also worked to the disadvantage of parties other than the Bolsheviks. The Kadets, a party of liberals, were easy to attack for being middle class and bourgeois and were soon banned. The Mensheviks and Social Revolutionaries found it difficult to publish their newspapers due to restrictions imposed by the Bolsheviks. The Left Social Revolutionaries, however, who had been given a role within the Bolshevik government in 1917 and 1918, were able to have some impact on policy. They had persuaded the Bolsheviks to reduce the use of terror when dealing with the peasants in order to requisition grain. Nonetheless, their days were numbered.

In March 1918 the Bolshevik Party renamed itself the Communist Party of the Bolsheviks and by 1921 all other parties were banned. The secret police were to enforce ruthlessly the ban on other political parties. After an attempt on Lenin's life in August 1918 there had been a swoop against the SRs. Fanny Kaplan, a woman with SR sympathies, was arrested on the spot. As she was almost blind it is difficult to believe she was the assassin but she provided a useful excuse to move against the SRs. In

1922 there was a wave of arrests of SR and Menshevik supporters but by this stage they had ceased to exist as organised parties.

Lenin had stated before coming to power that the proletariat was incapable of self-organisation. Therefore, the Communist Party would have to direct the Revolution on their behalf. For this purpose, Lenin argued that the dominance of the party was an essential requirement.

The establishment of central control over the party structure

It was not only groups outside the Bolshevik Party that were brought under control, the leadership was to ensure rigid central control was exercised over the party's own structure and members. When the Bolsheviks seized power the party organisation was chaotic but the leadership was to extend its control. Local branches were brought firmly under the control of the organisations at the centre of the party. All branches sent representatives to the party congress but power was delegated to the Central Committee. The Central Committee, made up of thirty to forty members, was the key decision-making body of the party until 1919. After 1919 this role was taken over by the Politburo, a smaller body of between eight and nine members who were elected by the Central Committee. In theory this structure seemed democratic – each body was elected by groups within the party. But in practice the leadership began increasingly to exercise control over the membership and this trend was helped by the strengthened role of the party secretariat, which the national leadership were to use to control the appointment of local party officials.

This centralising trend has often been cited as evidence of the authoritarian nature of Bolshevism which allowed Lenin to impose his will on the party. It is a view that needs to be challenged in two respects. First, Moscow found it extremely difficult to extend its full control to the most distant provinces where local officials continued to exercise power without too much central intervention. Secondly, recent research has shed a different light on the process of centralisation. Whilst not denying the trend towards authoritarianism, historians such as Robert Service (1997) have drawn attention to the attitudes of local party members who, in the chaos of the early years of the regime, actively welcomed greater direction from above. During the Civil War local party members were desperate for support.

Dealing with internal party dissent

The firm line taken against dissent within the party has been seen as an important step towards the increasingly dictatorial approach of Lenin. There were examples of factions within the party in the early years. In 1919, a group known as the Democratic Centralists developed, calling for changes to the party's structure. In 1920, the Workers' Opposition emerged in response to increased party control over workers' organisations in the factories. Although both of these groups were loyal to the Bolshevik cause and easily dealt with by the leadership, they illustrated a trend which could pose a danger in the future.

The ban on the formation of factions within the party was put forward by Lenin at the Tenth Party Congress of 1921. This measure, known as 'On Party Unity' was an attempt to impose the view of the leadership on the party. The death penalty could be used against those breaking this rule. Although Stalin was later to use the same rule against his enemies in the party, Lenin had introduced it when the Kronstadt Mutiny had shown that serious opposition to the party still existed and discipline was therefore required.

Party control over the state

The Bolsheviks had found the machinery of administration that had served the Tsarist regime in chaos when they came to power. Lenin had frowned upon traditional forms of government and the state administration that came with them. The Bolsheviks wanted to set up state organisations which served the interests of the Revolution. The All-Russian Congress of Soviets elected members of the Central Executive Committee, which exercised power on their behalf. Above the Central Executive Committee was the Sovnarkom, a council made up of commissars who directed policy areas. Thus, the state organisations mirrored those of the party (see table on p. 136). Lenin acted as both chairman of the Sovnarkom and a member of the Politburo. Yet it was the party structure that controlled decision-making; whilst the state became little more than an organisation of administrators. The decline of the state was indicated by the increasing infrequency of meetings of the Congress of Soviets, Central Executive Committee and the Sovnarkom. When leading Bolsheviks were members of both the Politburo and the Sovnarkom, it was to the latter that they sent their deputies. Another sign of the relative power of state and party was the decision in 1919 to make the secret police directly responsible to the Politburo.

The growth in the size of both party and state was to cause concern for some Bolsheviks. Trotsky was particularly critical of Lenin's system of administration. He saw the danger in the bureaucracy of both state and party becoming the 'masters rather than the servants' of the people. He also thought that the structures set up by Lenin would lead to the emergence of a dictator within the party. At the end of his life, Lenin started to share these concerns.

The use of terror

Lenin had stated that the party should not flinch from the use of terror in order to safeguard the Revolution and implement socialism. Thus he was

State institutions	Communist Party institutions
Sovnarkom The Council of People's Commissars. Elected by . . .	**Politburo** The key decision-making body made up of an inner group of party leaders. Elected by . . .
Central Executive Committee Co-ordinated all government administration and oversaw the law-making process on behalf of the Congress of Soviets. Elected by . . .	**Central Committee** In theory this was the key decision-making body in the party but this function was exercised by the Politburo on its behalf. Elected by . . .
All-Russian Congress of Soviets The supreme law-making body of the state. All laws had to be passed by this body. In practice it became a body that rubber-stamped laws drawn up by the party. Elected by members of all local soviets, in theory all those citizens who were engaged in 'useful work'.	**Party Congress** A body made up of representatives of local party branches. It discussed the general programme of the party.

The structures of party and state under Lenin.

able to justify his use of terror. The Cheka's powers were expanded during the Civil War so that counter-revolutionaries could be eliminated. Lenin and Trotsky agreed with the view of Dzerzhinsky, the head of the Cheka, that it was better to overkill than run the risk of being overthrown. Terror was to be used against class enemies although it was also directed against elements within the party, such as 'adventurers, drunkards and hooligans'. At the end of his life, Lenin seems to have developed an obsession over the use of terror. Letters he wrote in 1922 called for intensified repression against the Mensheviks, including the harmless historian Rozhkov. This seems to indicate that Lenin was developing his own, personal agenda for the use of terror.

The Soviet Constitution

The first constitution, introduced by the Bolsheviks in 1918, set up the Russian Socialist Federal Soviet Republic (RSFSR). The 'Russian' in the title was *Rossiiskaya*, a term used to describe a geographical area, rather than *Russkaya*, a term used to describe the Russians as an ethnic group.

This was a deliberate policy to welcome the other nationalities of the old Russian Empire into the new Soviet state. The Bolsheviks had to tread carefully when dealing with the national minorities, who had gained a taste of self-government during the Civil War. By 1923 the new Soviet Constitution was to show the Bolsheviks had gained the confidence to strengthen their hold over the outlying regions. In theory the Union of Soviet Socialist Republics (USSR) was a federal state but in practice it tightened the authority of the Communist Party based in Moscow. The Communist Party bodies in the various republics, such as the Ukraine, were firmly under the control of the central party structure. The Constitution was an important step in the centralisation of power in the Soviet state.

By 1924 the Communist Party had established a system of strong, central rule. This was an authoritarian state, justified by the Bolsheviks in terms of the need to establish a Dictatorship of the Proletariat in the face of enormous difficulties. The party saw itself as the vanguard of the Revolution taking on the role of organising the workers and steering a path towards a socialist state. The Civil War had revealed the serious threat posed by counter-revolutionaries and weakened the proletariat. The mass movement of people from the towns to the countryside during the Civil War had decimated the proletariat and left the Bolsheviks exposed. Lenin realised that in this situation authoritarian rule by the party was needed and circumstances pushed the Bolsheviks into a more ruthless and authoritarian approach than they had envisaged. These circumstances can be said to have militarised the culture of the party. That the Bolsheviks continued to rely on the use of terror showed their continued insecurity, as did the growth of an inflexible and authoritarian bureaucracy. These were instruments that were starting to be used to maintain a dictatorship of the party rather than a Dictatorship of the Proletariat.

Lenin would have been appalled at the idea of an individual emerging from the Revolution as a dictator but he was concerned that this could happen. His *Testament*, written in 1922, warned the party against this danger. The French Revolution of 1789 had been full of revolutionary hopes and ideals, only to see the emergence of Napoleon as a dictator. Lenin, himself, was a strong leader able to use his strength of personality to impose his will yet this does not mean he acted as a dictator for his own personal ends. One of Lenin's most important qualities was his devotion to the revolutionary cause to the point of obsession. Nonetheless, it was Lenin who put in place the party and state machinery that enabled a dictator in the form of Stalin to emerge.

HOW TOTALITARIAN WAS THE BOLSHEVIK REGIME UNDER LENIN?

The concept of totalitarianism was developed by US political scientists after the Second World War. It was an attempt to explain the nature of the dictatorships which had emerged in the 1920s and 1930s. The concept focused on a system developed to gain total control over the economic, social and political life of a nation and involved:

- state control of the entire economy
- the mobilisation of the population by the state to rid the country of enemies
- state control over all forms of communication
- the large-scale use of terror to supervise the population
- adulation of a single leader
- and the imposition of a single ideology.

In order to consider how far the Bolshevik regime can be considered totalitarian it is useful to judge it against these criteria.

State control over the entire economy. The Bolshevik regime undoubtedly extended government control over most aspects of economic life. The nationalisation of large sectors of industry gave the government unprecedented economic intervention. At the local level, however, the party did make compromises with factory workers after listening to their concerns. The concessions brought about under the NEP left important sectors of the economy, such as small-scale industry and trade, outside Soviet control. Bolshevik control over food production was also reduced under the NEP. The emergence of Nepmen, kulaks and 'bourgeois experts' was a tangible indication of the degree of freedom still present under the NEP.

The mobilisation of the population by the state to rid the country of enemies. The organisation of resources during the Civil War can be used as evidence to support Bolshevik actions in this respect. The measures of War Communism were designed to mobilise the population in the face of attack from class enemies in the form of the Whites. It would, however, be misleading to see this mobilisation as completely effective. The chaotic situation and sheer size of the task were factors which limited the Bolsheviks' ability to bring about full mobilisation.

State control over all forms of communication. This was certainly true in terms of the control achieved by the Bolsheviks over the communication of political ideas. Yet government intervention in popular culture and the arts was limited under Lenin due to more pressing concerns, such as the Civil War, and even by 1924 the Bolsheviks had not yet decided on a firm policy towards cultural life. Writers and artists were allowed some freedom in the choice of subjects for their work.

The large-scale use of terror to supervise the population. There is no doubt that the Bolsheviks made significant use of terror through the work of the Cheka. Yet it would be misleading to think that the Bolshevik regime did not enjoy a degree of popular support. The elections for the Constituent Assembly in 1917 had revealed support for the Bolshevik Party in the large industrial cities and amongst the industrial workers support remained high. The use of terror against class enemies was popular with some workers and peasants as it offered a chance to see old scores settled.

Adulation of a single leader. There is no evidence to accuse the Bolsheviks of raising Lenin to the status of a cult figure for political purposes until *after* his death.

The imposition of a single ideology. The centralisation of the party and the establishment of a one-party state support the accusation that there was an imposition of a single ideology. By 1924 Lenin had banned all other political parties and internal dissent within the Communist Party was restricted. Yet the survival, albeit in a restricted manner, of the Russian Orthodox Church provided an alternative to communist ideology. The same could be said of the survival of Islamic traditions in Central Asia.

Judged against these criteria, the Bolshevik regime clearly shows some of the features of totalitarianism yet there are important differences. The assumption that Bolshevik Russia was a powerful monolithic state needs to be challenged. The control of the Bolshevik Party was limited by the chaos caused by the Revolution and the subsequent Civil War. G. Yaney, in *The Urge to Mobilise* (1982) has shown the impact of Bolshevik decrees in the countryside to be less effective than previously thought and has drawn attention to regional variations in the implementation of central decrees. There were in fact significant limits to the power exercised by the Bolsheviks.

TO WHAT EXTENT HAD THE 'PILLARS OF TSARISM' BEEN REMOVED BY 1924 AND WHAT HAD REPLACED THEM?

The authoritarian nature of the Bolshevik regime has drawn comparisons with the system of autocracy under the Tsarist regime. Did the Bolsheviks bring about real change or was one repressive regime merely replaced by another?

The Bolshevik Government had been in power for nearly seven years when Lenin died in 1924. In that time it had tried to sweep away the remnants of the old order and establish the basis of a new system from which communism would develop. One measure of success is to examine the extent to which the Bolsheviks removed the 'pillars of Tsarism'; those instruments of control which had supported the old regime.

The Tsar. The Tsar had been removed from power in the February Revolution of 1917. The royal family was to remain a potential focus for the counter-revolutionaries until the Bolsheviks executed them at Ekaterinburg in July 1918. The death of the Romanovs marked an end to the chances of restoring autocracy in Russia. Autocracy was based on rule by one person, the Tsar. Without a parliament, this was a system where power resided solely with the Tsar. The concentration of power in one source has led to comparisons with the role of Lenin under the Bolshevik regime. Nevertheless these comparisons should not be taken too far. There were important differences between autocracy and Bolshevik rule:

- Russian autocracy was based on the assumption that the Tsar ruled by divine right, i.e. he was chosen by God. No such claim was ever made by the Bolsheviks.

- The position of Tsar carried responsibilities which were taken seriously by most rulers. The Tsar was the 'little father' of the Russian people whose role it was to protect the people from the worst excesses of exploitation. This paternalistic attitude was considered by the Bolsheviks to be patronising and meaningless. To the Bolsheviks the only way of ensuring the interests of the Russian workers were met was through a Dictatorship of the Proletariat and the development of socialism.

- Although the Tsar ruled with the help of his advisers and through the apparatus of the army, secret police, Church and bureaucracy, all power resided with the Tsar. Under the Bolshevik regime, despite the personal authority of Lenin, power rested in institutions that in theory represented the interests of the people.

The aristocracy had been the richest section of society, whose wealth was based on large landed estates. They had been stripped of the basis of their power by the Land Decree of 1917. Many had fled the country as émigrés both in 1917, after the Revolution, and in 1921 when the defeat of the Whites was imminent. Nonetheless, about 100,000 landowners from the aristocracy and gentry were still resident in the countryside in the mid-1920s. The amount of land they were allowed to keep after redistribution was often rather generous.

The bureaucracy of the former regime was hardly likely to contain many Bolshevik supporters but there were advantages for both sides in retaining a working relationship. The Bolsheviks were keen to use the expertise and specialist staff of the existing bureaucracy, at least until they could replace them with technically-trained party members. The civil servants and officials of the old regime were quick to see some of the advantages of holding positions of status in the new regime. These advantages were greater for those who joined the party.

The army of the Tsar had disintegrated to be replaced by a Red Army under Communist Party control. Yet beneath the surface there were some remnants of the old regime present. The return to a hierarchical system of authority after the initial period reinforced those values of discipline and obedience which had been part of the old army. The use of over 50,000 ex-Tsarist officers provided some degree of continuity.

The secret police. There was less continuity of personnel in the secret police. The Cheka was a new organisation recruited from Bolshevik members. However, there was clearly a degree of continuity in the methods used to rule the country. When the Cheka was replaced by the more bureaucratic OGPU the similarities with the Tsarist secret police, the Okhrana, became more noticeable. Both the Tsarist regime and the Bolsheviks relied on instruments of terror to bolster their governments.

The Church had seen its influence heavily curtailed by the Bolsheviks. As an integral pillar of the Tsarist regime, its fate was sealed by the collapse of the Tsarist government. The Church was separated from the state in 1918 and it lost its influence as a landowner when its estates were taken away without compensation. Clergymen were deprived of the vote and, to restrict the Church's hold over the people, all religious education outside the home was banned. The ideology of communism was to replace that of the Church. Lenin disliked all aspects of religion but he, like other leading Bolsheviks, was aware of the influence of religious symbolism and was prepared to use it in Bolshevik propaganda when required.

By 1924 the 'pillars of Tsarism' had been swept away although remnants of the old system remained beneath the surface. The Bolsheviks often reverted to the methods of the old regime e.g. terror and bureaucracy, dictatorship and authoritarianism. The fate of the Constituent Assembly showed parallels with that of the Duma under Nicholas II; both were representative bodies disbanded by government action. In fact, given the changes which had occurred to other social groups in Russia the Bolsheviks were in a minority position relying, like the Tsar, on a limited social basis of support. This situation had required practical compromises.

The industrial workers had suffered enormously due to the disruption of the Civil War and many had either joined the Red Army or fled back to the countryside. Between 1917 and the end of 1920 the number of factory workers had fallen from 3.5 million to 1 million. This had a severe impact on the party, which claimed to be representing this group. Conditions for the industrial workers were in many cases worse in 1924 than in 1914. Housing conditions were poor and a large reserve of unemployed workers kept wages low. Industrial workers resented the peasants who were seen as profiting from high food prices at the expense of the urban population. The War Communism had removed 'workers' control' of the factories and factory administration was once again hierarchical. Workers were to complain that the trade unions had become instruments of the factory managers, too occupied with dismissing and fining workers to protect their rights and improve their conditions. The division between the technical specialists, who continued to have status and authority, and ordinary operatives, who did not, was also a source of tension. The government was starting to be seen as the exploiters of labour in much the same way as the Tsar's government had been viewed before the Revolution.

The NEP did much to retain some influence for a section of the **middle classes**. Managers of factories were often those of the pre-revolutionary period and even some former-owners were given managerial positions. Although criticised by some Bolsheviks as 'bourgeois experts' their expertise was put to use by a government desperate to get the economy working again. The return of small-scale industry to private hands and the legalisation of private trade under the NEP led to the creation of a growing group of 'Nepmen'. This was a term of abuse used to refer to those, such as shop owners, traders, small-business people and kulaks who were able to profit from the NEP. The fact that this became such a divisive issue shows that the middle classes had not yet been completely destroyed.

The peasantry was the only social class to survive the Revolution more or less in its previous form. They had gained under the redistribution of land from the large estates and the mir had become a genuine peasant organisation. The Communist Party was weak in the countryside with only 0.13 per cent of villagers party members in 1922. This left the mir to be dominated by the village notables. There were divisions in the rural community: the kulaks were portrayed by the Bolsheviks as a group of richer, capitalist peasants but in practice they were only marginally better off than the poorer peasants. The biggest difference perceived by those in the villages was that between the peasants and urban society.

In 1924 it was still unclear what the Bolsheviks' 'New World' would look like. The old system had gone, leaving only remnants that were able to survive under the new regime. Bolshevik Russia was struggling to find a new identity. The Civil War had divided the party from its key supporters – the workers and the peasants – and the compromises made under the NEP had left a state of uncertainty. Perhaps more had been destroyed than created by 1924. One indication of this was the Bolsheviks' reliance on terror to maintain themselves in power. Traditional methods of control were relied upon. The fact that many leading Bolsheviks had become disillusioned indicates a failure to produce the sort of change originally envisaged. The Bolsheviks now had to come to terms with this reality.

SECTION 6

How important was the role of Lenin?

The creation and development of the world's first socialist state has attracted an enormous amount of attention by commentators and historians. Interpretations of Lenin and his achievements have been greatly influenced by the ideological nature of the Soviet state and historians have often been affected by their own values and attitudes. Lenin can be seen as someone who showed that it was possible to overthrow an existing power structure in the name of the workers. He is therefore seen as symbolising either a threat or an inspiration, depending on one's viewpoint. The stakes are high when assessing Lenin and as a result the debate has been particularly lively.

THE ROLE OF THE INDIVIDUAL: INTERPRETATIONS OF LENIN

The main schools of historical thought covered in Section 2 are all relevant in considerations of Lenin's role. There was, until recently, a general level of agreement amongst historians on the importance of Lenin in driving historical events. The area of disagreement tended to be over whether Lenin's achievements were generally positive or negative in their impact. Recent approaches have viewed Lenin in a relatively detached manner and have tended to see him more restricted by the circumstances he found himself in. Historians looking at the structures of Lenin's new state have focused less on the individual so that Lenin's significance is reduced by being placed within the wider context. In later years Lenin was used as a symbol of communism by the Soviet state and raised to the status of a god-like figure. On his death, his body was embalmed and placed in the mausoleum in Red Square to be visited by Soviet citizens (and foreign tourists!) in their millions. Lenin thus became a cult. What historians have been trying to do ever since is to find the human Lenin (a rounded individual – warts and all) by stripping away the manufactured god-like figure.

The Soviet school before 'glasnost'

Writers in the Soviet Union were, until the 1980s, actively involved in the process of turning Lenin into a symbol of the Revolution, someone who was above criticism. Lenin himself wrote extensively but his works reveal little of his own early background and give only a fragmentary picture of the man. His *Collected Works* (1920) are concerned largely with ideology and political issues. One of the earliest biographies of Lenin was written by Trotsky who saw the contribution of Lenin to the Revolution as crucial. This emphasis on the importance of Lenin ran contrary to the standard view of Marxists on the process of historical change, where individuals matter less than socio-economic forces. Lenin's wife, Krupskaya, wrote a biography of her husband in 1927 but it is strangely unrevealing, clearly showing signs of government censorship. After the death of Lenin in 1924 it became difficult for any Soviet citizen to criticise him. As the struggle for power developed, the rivals in the succession used Lenin's name, ideas and policies as a benchmark against which their own authority could be measured.

In the 1930s, when Stalin was in power, books on Lenin in the Soviet Union could be categorised as **hagiography**, works designed to encourage the worship of Lenin and his achievements. This suited Stalin's purpose of presenting himself as the legitimate and faithful successor to Lenin. Later Soviet leaders were also keen to continue this hero-worship in order to legitimise their own position and that of the party. Examples of this approach can be found in the official histories of the Soviet Union which were often written as school textbooks. The official biography by P. N. Pospelov (1963) described Lenin as an infallible and saintly leader. Other works talked of his genius and never-ending list of good qualities.

Soviet writers in the period of 'glasnost'

After the mid-1980s there was more freedom for Soviet writers to investigate the past and be more critical. This was a result of Gorbachev's policy of *glasnost* or openness, when greater freedom of speech was permitted. Yet it was Gorbachev's other policy of *perestroika*, with its emphasis on a mixed economy of both private and state enterprise, which led to a positive view of Lenin's NEP by Russian historians and commentators. Nonetheless, some writers were more critical, pointing to the excesses of the Civil War period and the arbitrary nature of terror. These more negative aspects were often attributed to individuals such as Dzerzhinsky and Trotsky rather than Lenin. The ruling against 'factionalism', which had the effect of quashing criticism within the party and making it less tolerant, could be levelled more directly at Lenin. Yet various writers have pointed to the fact that in Lenin's day critics appeared at party congresses and that there was some opposition in the Young Communist League which the government tolerated. According to many Soviet writers at the time of *perestroika*, Lenin was therefore a flexible and far-sighted genius who had introduced the NEP and struggled against both the creation of an all-powerful bureaucracy and the placing of more power into the hands of Stalin. As B. Oleinik stated in 1988, Lenin's greatest weakness was that he 'prepared us for the parliamentary road of development but he didn't live long enough'. Soviet writers could always justify faults and mistakes as due to the pressure of the desperate situation the Bolsheviks had found themselves in, although Selyunin (1987) was more critical of Lenin's use of force against 'counter-revolutionaries' and his policies towards the peasants during War Communism. G. Popov (1987) pointed out that Lenin understood that banning factions in the party could cause problems but that his measures to deal with this were ineffectual.

Other Marxist writers

Not all commentaries on Lenin from a Marxist viewpoint have come from Soviet writers. A range of books has been published by Marxists in the West, although not all have gone as far as J. B. S. Haldane, the British Leninist, who claimed that reading the works of Lenin had cured his stomach ulcer. Nevertheless, Marxist approaches in the West have tended to be positive. Christopher Hill's *Lenin and the Russian Revolution* (1947) is a good example of a favourable view of Lenin and his achievements. He saw the Russian leader as essentially democratic and humane. Hill was, of course, influenced by his own views of Marxism and it should also be remembered that he was writing at a time when Britain had just defeated Nazi Germany with the support of Soviet Russia. It is perhaps of no surprise that the Soviet Union was seen in a good light in the immediate aftermath of the Second World War.

Russian writers since 1991

With the collapse of the Soviet Union in 1991 Russian writers were given much more flexibility in their analyses of Lenin. The rejection of communism as a whole led writers to reject Leninism and the Bolshevik Revolution as either justified or inevitable. A 'mental' revolution took place that seemed to discard communist ideas and practice. Dmitri Volkogonov's *Lenin: Life and Legacy* (1994) was a valuable addition to the debate. Volkogonov was a professional soldier for most of his life and rose to the position of Colonel-General under Brezhnev and later took the post of Director of the Institute of Military History in Moscow. The importance of Volkogonov's work lies in the access he had to government files which were not available to Western historians: his career meant that he had inside knowledge of the Soviet system and how it operated. His book provoked a deeply divided debate. Its critical approach to Lenin was condemned by those who saw the end of the Soviet Union as a tragedy for the working people but praised by those who had come to see communism as irrelevant to the needs of Russia at the end of the twentieth century. Volkogonov was also very concerned with the future of Russia and aimed to show, through his book on Lenin, the dangers of radical politics and authoritarian governments. These concerns also mirrored the problems faced by Boris Yeltsin as Russian leader in the 1990s. Volkogonov wrote in 1993: 'Russia is trying to move onto a democratic and civilised path for the second time in the twentieth century. The first time was in February 1917. Then the weak inexperienced Russian democracy lost to the Bolsheviks. Now 75 years later, Russia has another chance to become a civilised society.' Clearly the past was being used to reflect on the present and options for the future.

Volkogonov's far more critical approach has been echoed in works produced by historians in the old Soviet republics outside Russia. As relatively new states they have been busy writing their own histories as part of the movement to find and assert their own identity. Within this context they see the old Soviet regime, based on Leninism, as the instrument by which they were oppressed.

The Liberal school

Early Western historiography of the course of the Revolution under Lenin was dominated by the Liberal school. They saw the role of Lenin as of central importance in determining the course of events, although in a negative way. Events were cited to prove the Liberal view of the Bolshevik Party as fundamentally undemocratic, ruthless and even evil. This view was coloured by the Bolshevik withdrawal from the First World War, which was seen as a betrayal of the Allied cause. The Bolsheviks' decision not to pay back loans to the West and to confiscate Western assets in Russia without compensation did little to improve the view of Lenin's government by those in the West. The terror unleashed during the Civil War went against those values of freedom of speech and human rights held so dear by Liberals. The sources used by historians in the years before the Second World War reinforced this view. A lot of reliance was placed on the memoirs of émigrés who had fled Russia, many of whom were members of the Russian aristocracy who feared they would lose all their wealth and status under the new regime. In the absence of Soviet sources, the works of P. Miliukov (*History of Russia*, 1932) and A. Kerensky (*The Russian Provisional Government*, 1961) were particularly influential. These writers encouraged an approach which focused on political leaders and their importance rather than on social and economic developments, which were much more difficult to investigate given the lack of contemporary archive material.

D. Schub's *Lenin* (1948) and B. Wolfe's *Three who made a Revolution* (1948) are early examples of the Liberal school of thought. Both drew on personal recollections: Schub had been a member of the Social Democratic Party in Russia before emigrating to the United States in 1908; Wolfe had known both Trotsky and Stalin although he had never met Lenin. Later works by those writing from the Liberal school include L. Schapiro. In *The Communist Party of the Soviet Union* (1964) Schapiro presented a very critical view of Lenin and drew attention to the links between Lenin's rule and that of Stalin. This view was challenged by M. Liebmann in *Leninism under Lenin* (1975), a much more sympathetic viewpoint which refuted the charge that Lenin laid the basis for the totalitarian regime of Stalin. To Liebmann, Lenin's authority did not rest on terror and this was an important difference with Stalin.

A Bolshevik painting showing Lenin in revolutionary pose.

Robert Daniels in *Red October, the Bolshevik Revolution* (1967) saw the role of Lenin as crucial to the Revolution. His 'wild gamble' to seize power in 1917 had a decisive impact on the course of the Revolution. In this respect, without Lenin there would have been no Bolshevik Revolution. Thus, as an individual, Lenin's personal role was of enormous importance. His intentions and ideas became powerful instruments for bringing about change. Historians who emphasise this are sometimes termed intentionalists.

Although the orthodox liberal view has been seriously challenged and some of its basic assumptions on the importance of individuals no longer hold up to scrutiny, many historians in the West still support this approach.

One exception to this approach was the massive study of the Russian Revolution by E. H. Carr (*The Bolshevik Revolution*, 1950-3). Although Carr's view of Lenin was not very positive, the main focus of his study was on broader historical trends and institutions rather than on individuals. The concentration on the development of party structures led Carr to draw comparisons with those features of the administrative system closely associated with Stalin. This work was an early example of the structuralist approach to the Russian Revolution.

The Libertarian school

To the Libertarian school, the Bolshevik Revolution and Lenin's actions in government marked an end to the freedom of the workers and peasants gained in February 1917. This view was put forward by writers on the extreme Left, especially by anarchists. They pointed to the formation of the Red Army on traditional hierarchical lines as an example of power being taken out of the hands of the workers' militia groups. The establishment of party control over the factories and the reduced role of the soviets and factory committees are also highlighted as evidence of how the Bolsheviks hijacked the Revolution for their own ends at the expense of the proletariat. Needless to say, writers from this school often represent the revolutionary groups, other than the Bolsheviks, that were present in Russia in 1917.

In the 1960s, the views of the Libertarian school were given weight by their association with the New Left. This period saw a growth in disenchantment with modern capitalist society, a feeling increased by the Vietnam War in America. The result was a more radical view of history by scholars caught up in this movement. To them all forms of oppression were to be despised. The focus of the Libertarian school has been on the industrial workers and the peasants and the degree of control they had over their own lives. M. Brinton's *Factory Committees and the Dictatorship of the Proletariat* (1975) is a good example of this. More recently, M. S. Shatz (1989) has examined the roots of Bolshevik authoritarianism to argue that the party was based on a class of 'intellectual workers' quite different from the mass of the industrial workforce. This class worked with the middle-ranking bureaucrats of the old Tsarist regime to establish control and form a class of its own. The result was the creation of a ruling class which treated the workers and peasants in much the same way as before. This division between the new Bolshevik government and the industrial workers was illustrated by the Kronstadt Mutiny. The main conclusion of this school is that the Revolution merely exchanged one set of oppressive rulers for another: the chance of liberty was lost.

The Libertarian school has been criticised for being too general and lacking evidence, with those historians adopting this approach often seen as radicals with axes to grind. Despite these criticisms the Libertarian school has been useful in moving the focus from Lenin the individual to the government and its relationship with social groups. Some of their views have carried more weight since the 1980s in the light of the conclusions drawn by revisionist historians.

The Revisionist school

The Revisionist school stemmed from dissatisfaction with both the Liberal and Libertarian views as well as the standard Soviet view. Less influenced by the concerns of the Cold War period when relations between the USA and the Soviet Union were poor, they tended to focus on social history. Their thrust has therefore been on the 'revolution from below', the role of the industrial workers and peasants, rather than on Lenin and the government. The other focus of the Revisionists has been on the structures of the Bolshevik Party and government. These approaches are often referred to as the **Structuralist school**. The greater availability of sources on social history and the workings of the party encouraged these lines of study. This has been largely due to the policy of *glasnost* in the mid-1980s and the later collapse of the Soviet Union.

What the Revisionists have done is to reduce attention on Lenin and see his role as of less importance. The 'genius' of Lenin has been cut down to size by looking at the situations and circumstances within which he operated. The Revisionist view is put forward by B. Williams in *The Russian Revolution 1917–1921* (1987), S. Fitzpatrick in *The Russian Revolution* (1982) and R. Service in *The Russian Revolution 1900–1927* (1986) and *Lenin: A Political Life* (3 volumes) (1990s). Service looked at the relationship between Lenin and his colleagues and his relationship with the party and its structure and concluded that Lenin's role has been exaggerated.

Revisionist historians are sometimes accused by Liberal historians of diverting attention from political leaders towards sociological issues in order to avoid judgements on what was, according to Liberal historians, a distasteful and brutal regime. Yet, as Revisionists have been keen to point out, Lenin's leadership and his government's policies can only be understood fully if you look at how they operated on the ground and this requires an examination of trends and developments in society.

Studies of the peasantry have shown a pattern of development which indicates a more limited government impact. Instead of bringing about change, Bolshevik policies on the redistribution of land after the Revolution merely confirmed what had, in many cases, already happened. G. Yaney in *The Urge to Mobilise: Agrarian Reform in Russia 1861–1930* (1982) has drawn attention to the fact that officials paid lip-service to Bolshevik calls for collective farms and took account of peasant demands and wishes when implementing policies. Thus, the student of Bolshevik

Russia should be aware that it is dangerous to assume that what the government decreed is what actually happened. Yaney also showed that the division between poor and richer peasants varied according to the area studied. The biggest differences amongst the peasantry were found in Western Siberia and the Urals. Such social histories are a useful reminder that in such a large country as Russia there are likely to be regional variations.

Studies of the industrial workers have similarly pointed to a more complex picture of reality than the simple carrying out of government orders. W. B. Husband's *Revolution in the Factory* (1990) has indicated that although the government could and did rely on force, factory officials implementing government orders could be understanding and sympathetic to workers' concerns. Absenteeism was tolerated and there were cases of workers being allowed to use factory equipment to make goods for bartering. It is clear that a lot of the products made in the factories were kept by the workers rather than handed over to the state.

The position of the 'Nepmen', those private traders who benefited from the NEP, has been studied by A. M. Ball in *Russia's Last Capitalists: The Nepmen 1921–1929* (1987). His work has shown that the Nepmen were severely restricted in how they could do business. Their profits were heavily taxed and they found it difficult to get credit and supplies from the state. The Nepmen included a lot of former business people who were now classed as potential 'enemies of the state' so they were unlikely to get government jobs and had to resort to becoming pedlars or selling what few goods they could make. The view of Nepmen as greedy, rich capitalists came from government propaganda not reality.

Histories of the urban classes in Russia tend to rely on evidence from Moscow and Petrograd. Whilst this is perhaps understandable given the size of the two cities and their dominance in the field of industry, it should not be assumed that other towns and cities followed the same pattern. This point is emerging through the work of Revisionist historians.

Conclusion

The ways in which historians have looked at the role of Lenin have clearly changed since the events of the Revolution itself. The emphasis on Lenin as the all-powerful leader (whether it is seen in a positive or negative light) has itself been consigned to history and the work of Revisionist historians has widened the focus to give a broader picture of the circumstances within which Lenin operated. The result has tended to reduce the importance of Lenin as an individual, leaving us with a sense of Lenin as a more fully rounded human being. We now have a more accurate portrait of a skilful political leader operating in exceptionally difficult circumstances.

Lenin
recuperating
after a series of
strokes, 1923.

Summary

The limits on Lenin's importance as an individual in the process of historical change

These limitations are highlighted by Revisionist and Structuralist historians:

- The February Revolution was a result of pressures which were not controlled by the Bolsheviks. 'There would probably have been a socialist regime in place in Russia by the end of the year whether or not Lenin had existed' (Service).
- Lenin was not in Russia for most of 1917. He returned from Switzerland in April, fled to Finland in July, came back in October. This limited his influence on the course of the Revolution in 1917.

- Lenin visited no city in Russia other than Petrograd in 1917.
- The idea that Lenin's writings and theories were keenly picked up by the Russian workers and peasants is clearly nonsense. *Pravda*, the Bolshevik newspaper only had a circulation of about 100,000 in 1917 and over half of these copies were distributed in Petrograd. For a country with a population of about 130 million, this was clearly of limited impact. Even as an orator, Lenin's skills were not well developed until after the Revolution.
- The influence of Trotsky and other Bolshevik leaders: Trotsky's work during the Civil War in organising the Red Army was vital to the survival of the regime; Dzerzhinsky's role as head of the Cheka was also of importance in consolidating the government.
- Lenin can be seen as changing certain policies because of pressure from the workers and peasants. The introduction of the NEP is a good example of this. This can be used to illustrate Lenin's lack of control over events.
- The pressure of party members, especially those who joined the party during the Civil War, had an influence on its attitudes. They tended to be less worried about the use of terror.
- The hierarchy of the party, especially in its use of bureaucrats from the former Tsarist regime, developed values of its own which favoured centralisation and rigid control. It took on a momentum of its own.
- From 1922 onwards Lenin was ill. He suffered a series of strokes and his health deteriorated. He was incapacitated for the last year of his life. Lenin's colleagues were already jockeying for position in preparation for the struggle to succeed him. Compare the photographs of Lenin on pages 148 and 152. They give two different views of Lenin.

Evidence which points to Lenin's importance as an individual
The importance of Lenin as an individual in the process of historical change is highlighted by the Liberal and intentionalist approaches:
- Lenin's decision to launch the Bolshevik seizure of power in October 1917 was of vital importance, as was his ability to persuade other Bolsheviks such as Zinoviev and Kamenev that the time was right to do so.
- He was highly committed and dedicated to the Revolution. Trotsky called Lenin 'The greatest engine-driver of Revolution'.
- Lenin did not want a coalition with other socialist groups, unlike many Bolsheviks.
- Lenin was able to persuade his party to accept the Treaty of Brest-Litovsk, in many cases against their better judgement.

- The decision to adopt the NEP was partly carried by Lenin's power of persuasion.
- Some difficult decisions were pushed through by Lenin by his threats of resignation. That this tactic worked clearly shows that other Bolsheviks considered Lenin to be indispensable.
- Lenin can be seen as a highly skilled politician (even if not a genius). He was able to relate theory to what the Russian workers actually wanted and was good at getting ideas across. His decision to seize power showed an acute sense of political timing. The acceptance of the Treaty of Brest-Litovsk and the introduction of the NEP showed Lenin to be not only a realist, but also a political strategist of the highest order.

SECTION 7

How and why did Stalin manage to secure power by 1929?

Historians have found the issue of Stalin's rise to power difficult to explain. It involved a complex sequence of events in which it has not been easy to discern Stalin's position and motives in the constant manoeuvring for power. Nonetheless, several factors have been identified which go some way to explain Stalin's rise to power:

- **Differences in personality.** Stalin's personality was better suited to the situation in which the party leadership found itself after 1924. Stalin was a shrewd and effective administrator, qualities which enabled him to outmanoeuvre his rivals. Trotsky, Zinoviev, Kamenev, Tomsky and Bukharin all had personality traits which prevented them making the most of the circumstances that arose after 1924; relationships were especially difficult between Stalin and Trotsky.
- **The situation in 1924.** The confused and uncertain atmosphere that prevailed after Lenin's death worked to the advantage of Stalin who, as General Secretary, had control over the party structures.
- **Stalin's positions in the party.** Stalin was able to influence the outcome of debates because of his powerful position as General Secretary. In this capacity he was also able to ensure his supporters were appointed to key posts within the party and could then outvote his rivals.
- **Structural changes in the party.** Stalin's supervision of the 'Lenin Enrolment' worked to his advantage. The membership recruitment drive of the 'Lenin Enrolment' increased greatly the number of workers in the Party. These new members were often poorly educated and politically naïve. They saw loyalty to the General Secretary as an important step in securing privileges as party members.
- **Lenin's funeral.** This event provided the opportunity for Stalin to ride on the wave of popular enthusiasm for Lenin and his achievements. It also highlighted Trotsky's tendency to make tactical errors as a political strategist. The contrast between Stalin as the chief mourner at the funeral and Trotsky, who was absent, was very telling.
- **The 'Lenin legacy'.** Stalin was able to manoeuvre himself into a position as the person most likely to continue the work of Lenin's legacy. This was to be a very powerful position given the cult of hero worship that had developed so quickly around Lenin.
- **Trotsky's attack on the party bureaucracy.** Trotsky's criticisms of the growing power of the bureaucracy were valid but they were unpopular with those party members who saw their newfound privileges and

status threatened. This highlighted Trotsky's lack of popularity and support within the party and contrasted with Stalin's position as head of the bureaucracy.

- **Differences over ideology.** Stalin was to defeat both the Left and the Right of the party during the 1920s over ideological issues. The relative importance of ideological differences compared to personality differences has been confused because they were to become closely entwined.

HOW IMPORTANT WERE IDEOLOGICAL DIFFERENCES IN STALIN'S RISE TO POWER?

Ideological differences arose over the future of the NEP and the call for Permanent Revolution. They were not, however, deep divisions which were irreconcilable but they did provide Stalin with opportunities to rid the party leadership of his opponents.

The defeat of the Left

The difference over the future of the NEP. The Left's call for an immediate abandonment of the NEP after 1924 was opposed by the Right who wished to keep it in place providing it continued to work. This disagreement was, it must be said, merely a difference of emphasis. The attitude of nearly all of the Bolshevik leaders was that the NEP would not last indefinitely. Few had any enthusiasm for the Nepmen, those private traders who were seen to have gained from the NEP. The Bolsheviks were also in agreement in sharing suspicions about the kulaks, the more prosperous peasants who seemed to represent a capitalist class of profiteers undermining the Revolution. What brought the differences over the NEP to the forefront was the unexpectedly rapid industrial growth of 1924-5. This led to a wave of optimism that the Revolution could, perhaps, move forward to socialism and the NEP could be ditched rather more quickly than had previously been anticipated. The Left was to partly represent this optimism. Yet in the political manoeuvring of the mid-1920s the issue was confused by the way these policy differences were linked to questions of Party loyalty. To call for a hasty abandonment of the NEP could be interpreted as a move away from the work of Lenin and a wrecking of his legacy.

The call for Permanent Revolution. Trotsky's call for Permanent World-wide Revolution was opposed by Stalin's policy of 'Socialism in One Country'. Again, this was an argument over priorities rather than irreconcilable divisions but it enabled Stalin to portray Trotsky as both disloyal and irresponsible. Trotsky's call for World Revolution was similar to that of the Mensheviks, a point Stalin was to make, and given

This picture was made from two separate photographs (look at the seating) in order to show Lenin and Stalin together.

Trotsky's Menshevik connections before the Revolution this again raised suspicions about Trotsky as a true Bolshevik Party man.

The defeat of the Right

After the removal of the Left in 1926 Stalin suddenly decided that the NEP must go. This switch to the views of the Left brought Stalin into disagreement with the Right. Was Stalin's manoeuvring a sign of his opportunism rather than a genuine ideological shift? After getting rid of the Left, did he then adopt their policies in order to remove the Right? This view is perhaps rather cynical. It must be remembered that Stalin had largely stayed out of the earlier debate between Preobrazhensky and Bukharin over the future of the NEP and instead of changing his views from the Right to the Left, Stalin may well have been undecided. The conflict with the Left was also intrinsically linked to Stalin's power struggle with Trotsky; it was not ideology which had provided the dominant division but personal ambition.

Conclusion

The Right, like the Left, had been defeated by Stalin's manipulation of the party organisation and structures. At face value the party divisions had been over issues of ideology but these differences should not be over-exaggerated. They were differences of emphasis and priority rather than irreconcilable splits. It is important to remember that the debate over the future direction of the Revolution was taking place in the context of a struggle for power and, in this situation, differences in ideological emphasis gave Stalin the opportunity to magnify divisions and remove those who stood in his way. The collective leadership which had been declared in 1924 at the death of Lenin was no more. Stalin had whittled away at the powers and position of the other main rivals until, by early 1929, he was in a dominant position. He was then free to implement the Five Year Plan and other policies unhindered.

INTERPRETATIONS OF THE RISE OF STALIN

Although no historian would suggest one single factor was responsible for the rise of Stalin, historians have differed in terms of which factor they see as the most important. Consequently, different schools of historians have placed the emphasis on varying factors, often according to the underlying philosophical principles of their particular school of thought.

The Liberal school

Historians of the Liberal school have, as would be expected, focused on the role of individuals and their personalities. According to this view, the main reason for Stalin's rise to power was his personal qualities. To Liberal historians, Stalin is seen as having grit, determination, shrewdness, craftiness and, of course, cruelty. This view has been presented in works such as B. D. Wolfe in *Three who made a Revolution* (1974) and in the psychological portraits of Stalin by R. Conquest in *Stalin* (1991) and R. Tucker in *Stalin as Revolutionary 1879–1929: A Study in History and Personality* (1974). Both Conquest and Tucker have highlighted Stalin's ruthlessness and double-dealing. They concentrate on the way in which Stalin deceived opponents and manipulated ideology for his own benefit. According to this approach Stalin's actions were merely devices to get rid of his opponents and make himself dictator.

By highlighting the role of personality, the Liberal school also provides an explanation of why the other Bolshevik leaders were unable to take advantage of the situation. The weaknesses of Stalin's opponents can be put down to deficiencies in their characters. Zinoviev is often presented as an unsavoury careerist, Kamenev as a politician without any coherent goal and Bukharin as politically shortsighted. These defects were to be crucial in their failure to use the situation after 1924 and to deal effectively with Stalin. No one was a match for the General Secretary. One major weakness which the Bolshevik leaders shared was in underestimating Stalin. In this respect, Zinoviev, Kamenev and Bukharin made the same mistake as Lenin who only realised Stalin's true character when he was ill and it was too late to rectify the situation.

The other personality was, of course, Trotsky who, according to the Liberal school, made tactical mistakes. His arrogance and indifferent personality led him to also underestimate Stalin as the 'grey blur' and 'outstanding mediocrity'. Trotsky's failure to organise his supporters and his absence at Lenin's funeral are emphasised as examples of his tactical failures.

When compared to the other Bolshevik leaders Stalin can be seen as the strongest personality and therefore it is the role of personality that is highlighted by the Liberal school to explain Stalin's rise to power. This approach is usually adopted in political biographies of Stalin where the focus is inevitably on the individual. The critical approach adopted by this school is largely due to the type of sources used. The Liberal school tended to rely on sources from émigrés, many of whom had suffered first-hand from Stalin's actions. This seemed good evidence to support the underlying principle that the intentions of individuals do matter in the process of historical change. This intentionalist approach found some agreement with the school of Soviet writers which emerged after 1930.

The Soviet school before 1985

After 1930, Soviet writers presented a view of the rise of Stalin that also focused on the role of personality but in a more positive light. When Stalin was still alive it was dangerous to do otherwise. History was turned into hagiography (biography that idolises its subject) as Stalin was praised as the leader who had saved socialism from both Trotsky and his supporters and the Right Deviationists such as Bukharin. This view was presented by G. F. Alexandrov in *Joseph Stalin: A Short Biography* (1947) who stated 'Foremost in the attack on the Party were Trotsky, that arch enemy of Leninism, and his henchmen'. E.Yaroslavsky went even further in *Landmarks in the Life of Stalin* (1942) by stating 'Long may he live and flourish, to the dismay of our enemies and to the joy of all working people – our own, dear Stalin'. This was clearly not a balanced account of Stalin's personality but it did present the official viewpoint until the mid-1950s when Nikita Khrushchev succeeded Stalin and introduced his policy of **destalinisation**. Khrushchev was more critical of Stalin and his 'errors' and this was reflected in the historiography which came out of the Soviet Union. When Leonid Brezhnev replaced Khrushchev as Soviet leader in 1964 destalinisation was slowed down and Stalin was ignored rather than criticised. This remained the general view in Soviet history books written thereafter until Gorbachev opened up the debate after 1985.

KEY TERM

Destalinisation
The policy of criticising aspects of Stalin's policies such as the use of terror. Destalinisation was launched in 1956 by Krushchev, Stalin's successor.

Russian writers since 1985

When Gorbachev implemented his policy of *glasnost* in 1985 the greater openness it fostered had an enormous influence on how Soviet writers could look at the past. Gorbachev had asked for ideas on how the socialist system could be improved and as a result there was a lot of criticism of the system Stalin had developed. By the party conference of 1988 most journalists and intellectuals had openly rejected Stalin's repressive dictatorship as a betrayal of the original spirit of the Revolution. It was convenient for many Russians to blame all the sins of the regime on one person rather than the system itself but as the Russian people moved towards a rejection of the Soviet system in its entirety the spotlight turned on Lenin and the establishment of the regime as the original sin. The rise of Stalin was seen as a result of the system created by Lenin and the attitudes and structures that developed with it. This trend has been echoed in the works of D. Volkogonov: *Stalin: Triumph and Tragedy* (1990) and *Trotsky: the Eternal Revolutionary* (1996) and mirrors, although from a different perspective, recent views from Western historians.

The Trotskyist approach

As a major player in the struggle with Stalin, Trotsky's viewpoint has a lot of value to the historian but he was obviously not an objective commentator. As someone who suffered at the hands of Stalin, he had an axe to grind.

Trotsky's perspective was from the angle of a Marxist. He saw Russia as not ready for revolution due to its economic backwardness. As a result the Revolution degenerated, the working class being too small in number to transform it into a true democratic dictatorship of the proletariat. Instead, according to Trotsky, it became a party-state machine of bureaucrats which ruled in its own interests. Stalin's success was due to the fact that he was a product of these circumstances brought about by the NEP; his actions were part of the process whereby the bureaucrats consolidated their position at the expense of the Revolution. In Trotsky's own words: 'All the worms are crawling out of the upturned soil of the manured Revolution'.

Trotsky's views were presented through books written whilst he was in exile and include *My Life* (1931) and *The Revolution Betrayed* (1937). Despite his obvious bias, Trotsky was able to present his argument making use of valuable inside knowledge. His recollection of some events is rather selective and some points made are unconvincing; for example, the reason given for not attending Lenin's funeral (Stalin had not informed him of the date) is weak. Nonetheless, for all its limitations, Trotsky's argument has formed the basis of much of the Revisionist work which has moved the emphasis away from the personality of Stalin to the structures and social context within which he operated.

The Structuralist approach

In the West, the standard liberal view of the importance of Stalin's personality was challenged in the 1960s and 1970s by Structuralist historians. This approach sees Stalin's rise to power as a triumph of the party organisation rather than of the individual, with the emphasis on the centralisation of policy into the hands of the party. The party administration started to replace the government and administration replaced politics. This was a direct response to the growth of responsibilities taken on by the party as the machinery of the state was enlarged. In this structure the centre of power became the Secretariat and at its head the General Secretary. It was therefore Stalin's position as General Secretary which was the key factor in the enormous power and influence attached to this role. Attention has been drawn to the trend of appointment replacing election within the party and this was crucial in explaining why Stalin was able to win votes, if not arguments, because the party officials had often been put in place by him.

Structuralist historians have indicated that Stalin's power was aided by the attitudes and ethos that developed within the party. The old values of the Tsarist bureaucracy of lack of initiative, boorishness and respect for authority were reinforced in the new system by not only the use of ex-Tsarist civil servants but also by purges which removed those who showed signs of disloyalty.

The Structuralist viewpoint was presented by E. H. Carr in *The Bolshevik Revolution* (1950–3), O. A. Narkiewicz in *The Making of the Soviet State Apparatus* (1970) and L. Schapiro in *The Origins of the Communist Autocracy* (1955). The value of the Structuralist approach is that it draws attention to the structures within which Stalin, and his rivals, had to operate. The increase in available sources from the Soviet archives since the mid-1980s has enabled historians to look in more depth at the working of the party structures, especially at lower and regional levels. This trend has led some Structuralists to develop their ideas in a slightly different direction by examining the history of the party.

The party history approach

This approach has been built on the Structuralist viewpoint by examining trends within the Bolshevik Party and looking at the growth of the party and its structures under Lenin. In *What is to be done?* (1902) Lenin had stated that the working class could never carry through a revolution unaided. It would require an organised party to guide the Revolution on behalf of the workers. This party would, according to Lenin, need to be organised, disciplined and centralised. Historians looking at the party's history have found these qualities in evidence since October 1917 and even before the seizure of power. They draw attention to Lenin's lack of tolerance when faced with the development of factions. According to this viewpoint, Stalin *was* the legitimate heir of Lenin in that Stalin's rise was based on a party structure that Lenin had put in place and that Stalin had merely used.

The party history approach has been put forward by G. Gill in *The Origins of the Stalinist Political System* (1990) and R. Service in *The Bolshevik Party in Revolution: a study in organisational change 1917–23* (1979). As well as making use of a wider range of sources this approach has been valuable in highlighting the elements of continuity in Bolshevik history.

The ideological approach

The more traditional view that Stalin was an evil schemer, as presented by the orthodox Liberal school in the West, has also been challenged by those historians who see matters of ideology and the debate over the NEP as more than a disguise for Stalin's personal ambition. This viewpoint has been put forward by E. H. Carr in *The Russian Revolution from Lenin to Stalin 1917–1929* (1979) and M. Lewin in *Political Undercurrents in Soviet Economic Debates from Bukharin to the Modern Reformers* (1974). Historians adopting the ideological approach stress that the struggle between Trotsky and Stalin was over the crucial issue of the future direction of the Revolution. This debate was set within the context of Lenin's retreat to the NEP and his failure to lay down clearly an indication of the life span of the NEP. To historians of this school the Left's view that the NEP should be ditched as soon as possible can be seen as a recipe for civil war between the peasants, who had gained under the policy, and the industrial workers who resented the concessions of the NEP. The Right's view of maintaining the NEP could, on the other hand, be seen as likely to lead to a restoration of capitalism due to its toleration of private enterprise. Stalin's position in this debate was therefore not that of an opportunist but of a practical politician balancing between two extremes. Thus, Stalin was prepared to keep the NEP while it worked but when it got into crisis he saw rapid industrialisation as the solution. Stalin's attack on Trotsky's notion of Permanent Revolution could also be seen as the action of a practical politician worried about the possibility of the Soviet Union getting involved in a war it was ill-equipped to fight.

The ideological approach does draw attention to the issues around which the struggle for power centred but many historians of the Liberal school criticise it for underestimating the role of personality and presenting Stalin in too positive a light. Liberal historians who saw communism as a threat to the Western system of liberal democracy preferred the image of a Soviet leader who was unprincipled and manipulative. The ideological approach has, however, received support from some of the Revisionist work undertaken since the mid-1980s.

The Revisionist school

With the release of more historical sources from the mid-1980s onwards, the traditional views of the rise of Stalin have been challenged with the emergence of Revisionist historians. The main thrust of the Revisionists has been an examination of social factors and changes in cultural attitudes and values. The wealth of sources available since *glasnost* has made this area of study much more viable. S. Fitzpatrick in *The Civil War as a formative experience* (1985) stresses the expansion of the party during the Civil War and how this affected its attitudes. The Civil War led to a need for authoritarianism and discipline in the party in order to ensure the effective use of resources during the war. The new members who joined the party at this time took on the military values which were reinforced by the war situation.

Social change has also been highlighted in other studies, such as in W. Chase's *Workers, Society and the Soviet State 1918-1929* (1987), which examine the Lenin Enrolment of 1924 and emphasise how it transformed the composition of the party. In order to control this huge growth in membership, obedience was encouraged rather than debate. This trend worked to the advantage of Stalin who as General Secretary controlled the party bureaucracy. With the influx of new members the gap between the rank and file of the party and the leadership increased. This was a concern which Stalin recognised and the attacks on both Trotsky and the Right of the party can be seen as attempts to gain the support of party members. Trotsky's criticism of the growth of the party's bureaucracy was a threat to the newly gained privileges of its members; Stalin's campaign against Trotsky was therefore popular with the party rank and file. By attacking the Right and moving away from the NEP, Stalin was able to gain support from the industrial workers and party members who wished to see an end to those remnants of the old system, such as the Nepmen, who posed a possible threat to their position.

The value of these Revisionist studies is in their use of social history to examine events from the perspective of the ruled rather than the rulers. The Revisionist school is, however, criticised because it tends to present Stalin as a puppet of social forces in the party rather than someone who had control over events. In this sense the Revisionist approach challenges the intentionalist assumption that individuals do matter in the process of historical change.

Conclusion

Although historians from the Liberal school focus on the personality of Stalin, it is evident that Stalin's personality cannot be divorced from the world he operated in. The Structuralist and Revisionist approaches have highlighted the context within which Stalin had to work. This context included important changes which were taking place in the party and society in general. Stalin may not have possessed the power to control events which was assumed by the orthodox Liberal school but he was able to tap into values and attitudes which had surrounded Bolshevik rule since 1917. The greater availability of sources since the opening up of archives after 1985 has provided historians with the ability to examine a wider range of factors with greater validity.

Summary of interpretations of the rise of Stalin

Key issue: How important was the role of personality in the rise of Stalin?

The Liberal school

VIEW:
- Focuses on the importance of individual personalities.
- Sees Stalin as a manipulator who rose to power by deceiving his opponents.

WHY:
- Relates to the underlying philosophy of the intentionalist approach to history, i.e. individuals can influence the course of history.
- Heavy reliance on the evidence of those who suffered at the hands of Stalin.
- Put forward by Liberal historians in the West to whom communism was intrinsically evil.

VALUE:
- Draws attention to the role of Stalin and other individuals.

The Soviet school before glasnost (1985)

VIEW:
- Saw Stalin's role as being of some influence within the context of socio-economic forces highlighted by Marxist perspective.

WHY:
- Related to standard Soviet view based on Marxism.
- Positive/negative view of Stalin depending on Soviet leader in power at the time of publication. Hagiography under Stalin, more critical under Khrushchev – both views for the propaganda purposes of the regime at the time.

VALUE:
- Highlights the importance of socio-economic changes leading to the rise of Stalin.
- But view of Stalin related to political factors rather than evidence.

Russian writers since 1985
VIEW:
- Tend to see the rise of Stalin as an inevitable result of authoritarian trends in the party.

WHY:
- Related to greater freedom of views after *glasnost*.
- Promoted by the rejection of the Soviet system and communism since 1991.

VALUE:
- Presents the view of those most affected by the legacy of Stalin.
- Makes use of a lot of new material previously unavailable in the West.

The Trotskyite school
VIEW:
- Stalin was a product of his circumstances. He represents a conservative reaction by bureaucrats sacrificing the Revolution for their own interests.

WHY:
- Relates to Marxist approach of examining the importance of socio-economic change.

VALUE:
- Trotsky experienced the rise of Stalin first-hand.
- But his failure to defeat Stalin coloured his view.

The Structuralist and party history approaches
VIEW:
- Sees the rise of Stalin as a product of the structures of the party. The party history approach sees continuity in the structural framework of the party since Lenin.

WHY:
- Related to the challenge to the dominant Liberal school in the West in the 1960s and 1970s.

VALUE:
- Focuses on the role of party structures during the rise of Stalin.

The ideological approach

VIEW:

- Emphasises the importance of ideology in Stalin's rise to power. Stalin was not driven by personal ambition but by practical and ideological reasons.

WHY:

- Part of the challenge to the more critical view of Stalin as a schemer for personal power presented by the Liberal School.
- Focuses on ideology as a factor, moving attention away from Western, stereotyped views of Stalin.

The Revisionist school

VIEW:

- See the rise of Stalin as due to social and cultural changes in the party membership. Stalin, the individual, is less important, merely representing social trends.

WHY:

- Relates to the increased use of sources available since *glasnost*, making social history more valid.

VALUE:

- Focuses on the influence of rank and file party members in shaping historical developments.
- But downplays the role of Stalin.

A2 ASSESSMENT: THE RUSSIAN REVOLUTION AND THE ESTABLISHMENT OF BOLSHEVIK POWER

Historiography

A consideration of different historical approaches to topics is an important skill for the student of history to develop. To begin with you may find historiography difficult because it requires you to know the wider context of influences on historical writing which often fall outside the period you are studying. For example, interpretations of Lenin have been influenced by events such as the Cold War and the fall of the Soviet Union, both of which occurred after the 1920s. Despite its challenges, historiography adds another level of understanding to studying topics, and the awareness that historians differ in their views and that the way they approach the past is changing all the time makes history especially exciting.

Evaluating historical perspectives

As a student of history you will be expected to consider the views of historians, to compare and contrast their arguments and assess their value. It is useful to think of the following aspects when you read extracts from the works of historians:

- What is the main **thrust** of the source? (i.e. what is it saying?)
- What **evidence** is being used by the author to develop the argument? (e.g. does the author rely on letters, conversations or personal accounts?) How is the evidence being used?
- What **angle** does the author take? (i.e. does the author focus on one particular angle and neglect others?) It is worth remembering that two historians from the same school of history may look at the same issue from different angles.
- The **background** of the author (i.e. has the nationality, date and other background factors affected the way in which the author sees the issue?).
- The **perspective** of the author (i.e. which approach does the historian seem to be taking and what school does he or she belong to? How have the underlying principles of this perspective affected the way in which the author has approached the topic?)

Explaining *how* historians agree/differ should be seen as a building block for moving on to consider *why*. This is what will usually be expected in high quality answers.

Most of the questions you will be working on will revolve around these points. Answers should always make close reference to the extracts you are asked to consider and this is best achieved by direct quotation of short phrases to support the points you wish to make. Comments such as 'see lines 8–12' are too vague and are unlikely to be rewarded.

Using historiography in essays

An understanding of historiography can be used to support and develop standard essays as well as more specific tasks. History is a subject which, by its very nature, involves extensive reading and in order to make maximum use of the material you have studied it is important to consider issues of historiography which are reflected in it. This will deepen your understanding of the topic and make you more competent as a historian.

When writing an essay it can be useful to refer to different historiographical perspectives and approaches. This shows an awareness of different interpretations and can demonstrate that you have engaged in wider reading. For essays specifically geared to historiography an awareness of historiographical issues will be essential. Nonetheless, there are several pitfalls to avoid.

a) Try to avoid a seemingly endless list of historians' names and their books. 'Name-dropping', in itself, is of limited use and examiners are well aware that students have often never read the books themselves but are merely regurgitating learnt lists of names. It is more important that you show an awareness of the different perspectives even if you have never read the books themselves and cannot even remember the names of historians involved. Showing an **understanding of the perspectives** is a higher level skill more likely to score marks.

b) Take care in quoting from historians. A statement by a historian can be useful in summing up a relevant point or as illustrating a factor but they should be used sparingly. It is never advisable to use long quotations, especially in exam answers, as the reward rarely compensates for the effort involved in learning the quote or the time taken to copy it out. Short, sharp quotes are preferable but think carefully about the purpose of the quotation. Just because a historian states something does not make it a fact. In other words, be careful not to confuse opinion with fact.

c) Referring to different interpretations by historians can often result in a lapse into description rather than using them as a tool of analysis to develop your argument. For example, the answer that falls into outlining what historian A states and then goes on to what historian B states is not using the material effectively. It is much better to **state whether you agree or disagree with the perspectives** covered and **why**. Writing historiographical essays usually requires you to explain the different perspectives and to assess their value. Ensure that you evaluate the different approaches by relating historians to their wider context and philosophical views.

For example, consider the evidence they have used, the period they were writing in and the values which have influenced them. This will enable you to show your skills in evaluation and assessment and therefore gain more marks than a merely descriptive answer, however detailed.

Questions with examiner's comments in the style of OCR

Source A:

The first steps of economic reorganisation were very moderate. There was very little nationalisation, except where active resistance was encountered. For example, the banks were left alone for two months and were only seized when they refused to lend money to the government. Heavy industry and private railways were not nationalised until June 1918, and then quite explicitly, on pragmatic grounds. Lenin's immediate aim was, as he said, 'a sort of state capitalism'.

For the War Communism period, he sometimes spoke of 'socialism' in being. Later, after the introduction of NEP, it could hardly be called 'socialism' and although he still sometimes referred to 'state capitalism', that lacked appeal. So the usual usage became just 'Soviet Society', a term without specific meaning. His famous phrase 'Communism is nothing but Soviet rule plus the electrification of the entire country' equally lacks Marxist content.

From R. Conquest, *Lenin* (1972).

Source B

Was War Communism a response to the war emergency and to collapse, or did it represent an all-out attempt to leap into socialism? I have already suggested that it could be both these things at once. Perhaps it should be said that it meant different things to different Bolsheviks, and this is an important element in our understanding of the about-turn of 1921. Some felt that the days of 1918–20 were not only heroic and glorious days of struggle, leading to victory against heavy odds, but were also stages towards socialism or even the gateway to full communism. [The NEP] seemed to them a betrayal of the revolution. Others saw the necessity of the retreat, but were above all concerned with limiting its consequences and resuming the advance at the earliest date.

From A. Nove, *An Economic History of the USSR 1917–1991* (1992).

Source C: The official view of the Soviet government

War Communism had been an attempt to take the fortress of the capitalist elements in town and countryside by assault, by a frontal attack. In this offensive the Party had gone too far ahead, and ran the risk of being cut off from its base. Now Lenin proposed to retire a little, to retreat for a while nearer to the base, to change from an assault of the fortress to the slower method of siege, so as to gather strength and resume the offensive.

From *The History of the Communist Party of the Soviet Union* (Short Course) (1941).

Questions

1 How far, and for what reasons, does the author of Source A agree with that of Source B in his explanation of changes in the economic policy of the Bolsheviks?

Examiner's comments: This type of question is designed to test your ability to compare historical sources both in terms of their content and their relative value. Answers will be expected to show close reference to the sources and a consideration of the overall perspectives of the authors. The authors of the sources may be unfamiliar to you and you should not worry about this. You will be expected to use clues in the extracts to come to a reasoned conclusion about the perspective adopted. A typical mark scheme for this type of question would be as follows:

LEVEL 1: A simple response with little or no relevant reference to the sources.

LEVEL 2: A developed response with reference to both sources. Answers will focus on the content of the sources rather than the overall perspective of the authors. To get to the top of this band there should be reference to areas of agreement and disagreement.

LEVEL 3: Developed explanation, with commentary, on the perspectives of the authors to assess the extent of agreement and the reasons for this.

The author of Source A emphasises 'pragmatic grounds' for economic policy changes. This finds some agreement with the author of Source B, 'a response to the war emergency and ruin', 'the necessity of retreat'. But Nove (Source B) also acknowledges that for some Bolsheviks War Communism was 'a leap into socialism', 'gateway to full communism' and that they 'wanted to resume the advance at the earliest date'. These differences might be explained by date: Nove is writing after the collapse of the USSR and will have had access to more sources, especially those relating to rank and file party members, than Conquest, writing in 1972. Conquest is writing from the more critical perspective of a liberal historian; Nove is writing from the more detached perspective of an economic historian, less concerned with individual leaders.

2 By reference to its origin and content, assess the usefulness and reliability of Source C to an historian studying the change from War Communism to the NEP.

Examiner's comments: This question is attempting to test your skills in evaluating a source for usefulness and reliability by a consideration of both origins and content. A mark scheme for this type of question would be as follows:

LEVEL 1: Simple response which focuses on content of the source.

LEVEL 2: Developed response with reference to both content *and* origins although this may be unbalanced.

LEVEL 3: A developed explanation which addresses both content and origins in some depth and provides a reasoned assessment of both usefulness and reliability.

Source C is useful in terms of **content** because it gives an insight into how policy changes were justified by the Soviet government to its own people, 'to retreat so as to gather strength'. The language used in the source is also useful as an illustration of the Soviet government's tendency to portray policies in a militaristic manner in order to appeal to those party members who had experienced the Civil War. These militaristic values would be very familiar to the Soviet population during the 1930s, with Stalin's push for industrialisation and later involvement in the Second World War. The **origins** of the source indicate that it needs to be treated with caution. This is the official view, issued in retrospect. It does not necessarily reflect the views of all party members, including some in the leadership, such as Bukharin, who objected to the NEP when it was introduced. Thus, its reliability as information on party views towards the NEP in 1921 is limited.

> **3** To what extent, and for what reasons, was Lenin able to adapt Marxist theory to the situation in Russia in 1917?

Examiner's comments: This is an essay question testing your ability to present an argument in response to the specific demands of the question. Factual information about the topic will be required to develop a convincing and reasoned argument. Factual knowledge that is not related directly to the focus of the question is unlikely to score a high mark. In order to achieve the highest bands some evaluation of different interpretations is expected. A typical mark scheme would be:

LEVEL 1: The answer is seriously flawed, e.g. a reasonably accurate narrative description with no real attempt to relate it to the specific **or** a response, supported by inadequate material.

LEVEL 2: Mainly descriptive, but has some relevant links to the question although this may be limited to the conclusion.

LEVEL 3: The answer shows an attempt to argue but this is within a largely descriptive framework. There may be a lot of information but the commentary is limited in scope and extent.

LEVEL 4: Most of the answer is focused on the question set and secure detail is applied to the demands of the question. The answer may be unbalanced but most aspects are addressed. There may be lapses into description but there will be a **sustained relevant commentary**.

LEVEL 5: A **clearly-focused** answer to the specific question which integrates a direct relevant argument with secure, well-selected evidence. All aspects of the question will be addressed although development of some may be limited.

LEVEL 6: A well-developed argument with a broad use of evidence and a wide perspective on the question. Shows evidence of widereading and applies it in an analytical manner. A sustained conceptual approach.

Question 3 requires an answer which addresses both 'to what extent' and 'for what reasons'. Detailed knowledge of both Marxist theory and Lenin's ideas is needed here (with reference to appropriate literature) but it must be used to address the two instructions in the question. An explanation of how the situation in Russia required an adaptation to Marxist theory will be expected. High level answers will consider whether it was possible to adapt Marxism to a rural-based economy and society, such as existed in Russia in 1917.

> **4** Consider the arguments for and against the claim that practical difficulties prevented Lenin from implementing communist ideology.

Examiner's comments: This question is designed to test your ability to assess different interpretations and the evidence for them. It is expected that you will come to a reasoned assessment of their relative merits. A knowledge of the most important interpretations and different schools of thought will be expected. A mark scheme for this type of historiographical essay would be:

LEVEL 1: Able to describe different interpretations of historical issues to show an awareness of how they differ.

LEVEL 2: Shows an awareness of different historical interpretations and offers some explanation of these differences based on their use of evidence.

LEVEL 3: Shows an awareness that different historical interpretations relate to the concerns, attitudes and values of the historians involved at the time of writing to provide evaluation of the interpretations.

LEVEL 4: Able to provide an explanation and full evaluation of different historical interpretations. Able to assess the relative value of different perspectives to make a reasoned, independent judgement about the inter-relationship between historians and the issues they are studying.

This question requires a consideration of the different interpretations of Lenin's achievements. The debate over Lenin's motives needs to be covered. Was Lenin a realist, adapting policies in the light of practical circumstances? Or did he abandon communist ideology to pursue a more personal agenda to keep himself and the Bolshevik Party in power at any cost? Knowledge of the various perspectives of different schools will be required, from the negative interpretation of the Liberal school to the more positive approach of Soviet writers. For higher marks, an evaluation of these different approaches would be needed.

BIBLIOGRAPHY

There are many books relevant to a study of Lenin and the Russian Revolution, the following being particularly useful:

E. Acton, *Rethinking the Russian Revolution* (Edward Arnold, 1990)
V. Andrle, *A Social History of Twentieth Century Russia* (Edward Arnold, 1994)
A. Bullock, *Hitler and Stalin: Parallel Lives* (HarperCollins, 1991)
E. H. Carr, *The Russian Revolution from Lenin to Stalin 1917–29* (Macmillan, 1979)
R. Charques, *The Twilight of Imperial Russia* (OUP, 1958)
P. Condren, 'Soviet Foreign Policy 1917–34' in *Modern History Review* (Feb 1990)
R. Conquest, *Red Empire* (Weidenfeld & Nicolson, 1990)
J. Daborn, *Russia: Revolution and Counter Revolution* (Cambridge University Press, 1991)
S. Fitzpatrick, *The Russian Revolution* (Opus, 1994)
G. Freeze (ed.), *Russia: a History* (Oxford University Press, 1997)
G. Hosking, *A History of the Soviet Union* (Fontana, 1992)
M. McCauley, *The Soviet Union* (Longman, 1993)
J. Milner, *Russian Revolutionary Art* (Oresko, 1979)
A. Nove, *An Economic History of the USSR* (Penguin, 1992)
R. Pipes, *The Three Whys of the Russian Revolution* (Pimlico, 1995)
C. Read, *From Tsar to Soviets: The Russian People and their Revolution* (UCL Press, 1996)
C. Read, 'The Cultural Intelligentsia' in R. Service (ed.), *Society and Politics in the Russian Revolution* (St Martin's Press, 1992)
R. Service, *A History of Twentieth Century Russia* (Penguin, 1997)
S. A. Smith, *Red Petrograd* (Cambridge University Press, 1983)
R. Stites, *Russian Popular Culture: Entertainment and Society Since 1900* (Cambridge University Press, 1992)
D. Volkogonov, *Trotsky: the Eternal Revolutionary* (HarperCollins, 1996)
D. Volkogonov, *The Rise and Fall of the Soviet Empire* (HarperCollins, 1998)

The following websites contain material relevant to the Russian Revolution:

http://www.marxists.org/archive/lenin/index.htm (Contains archive of material by Lenin)
http://www.marxists.org/archive/marx/index.htm (Contains archive of Marx's works)
http://www.anu.edu.au/polsci/marx/classics/trotsky.html (Archive of Trotsky's works)

http://www.fbuch.com/leon.htm (Information on Trotsky)

http://www.fbuch.com/posters.htm (Visual material on the Russian Revolution)

http://hsc.csu.edu.au/modhist/courses/2unit/twencent/russia (Articles on the Russian Revolution)

http://www.spb.ru/imperator/index.en.html (Material on Nicholas II)

http://www.fordham.edu/halsall/mod/modsbook39.html (Contains sources on Lenin)

http://kuhttp.cc.ukans.edu/kansas/cienciala/342/ch2.html (Articles on the Revolution and the Civil War)

To help you get the grades you deserve at AS and A Level History, you'll need up-to-date books that cover exactly the right options and help you at exam time.

So that's precisely what we've written.

How to Pass AS Modern World History   0 435 32752 6

- What your exam board is likely to ask you - and how to do it!
- What you need to know to pass your exam.
- Confidence-boosting preparation that really works.

The Heinemann Advanced History series

The English Reformation 1485-1558
0 435 32712 7

The Coming of the Civil War 1603-49
0 435 32713 5

England in Crisis 1640-60
0 435 32714 3

Poverty and Public Health 1815-1948
0 435 32715 1

Britain 1815-51: Protest and Reform
0 435 32716 X

The Extension of the Franchise, 1832-1931
0 435 32717 8

Lenin and the Russian Revolution
0 435 32719 4

Stalinist Russia
0 435 32720 8

Germany 1848-1914
0 435 32711 9

Germany 1919-45
0 435 32721 6

The USA 1917-45
0 435 32723 2

Civil Rights in the USA 1863-1980
0 435 32722 4

European Diplomacy 1870-1939
0 435 32734 8

The Reign of Elizabeth
0 435 32735 6

The Cold War
0 435 32736 4

Liberalism and Conservatism 1846-1905
0 435 32737 2

The European Reformation
0 435 32710 0

Russia 1848-1917
0 435 32718 6

France in Revolution
0 435 32732 1

Spain 1474-1700
0 435 32733 X

Mussolini and Italy
0 435 32725 9

F225

To see any title FREE for 60 days or to order your books straight away call Customer Services on 01865 888080.   S 999 ADV 08